D0245074

OBSERVING
THE COUNTRYSIDE
AND SEASHORE

OBSERVING
THE COUNTRYSIDE
AND SEASHORE

LESLIE JACKMAN

ILLUSTRATIONS BY
JAYNE NETLEY

Bloomsbury Books
London

FRONTISPIECE:
The heron. How close can you approach this wily, shy and alert bird?

TITLE PAGE:
A baby thrush, feathers fluffed for warmth.

To Lynne, who inspired the book.

First published in Great Britain 1990 by
Webb & Bower (Publishers) Limited
5 Cathedral Close, Exeter, Devon EX1 1EZ

Designed by Peter Wrigley

Text Copyright © 1990 Leslie Jackman
Illustrations Copyright © 1990 Jayne Netley

This edition published 1993 by
Bloomsbury Books, an imprint of
The Godfrey Cave Group
42 Bloomsbury Street, London WC1B 3QJ
under licence from Webb & Bower Ltd 1992.

ISBN 1-85471-079-6

Text set in Old Style

Typeset in Great Britain by Keyspools Ltd, Golborne, Lancs

Colour and mono reproduction by Mandarin Offset, Hong Kong

Printed and bound in Great Britain by
BPCC Hazells Ltd
Member of BPCC Ltd

CONTENTS

INTRODUCTION

*It is enough to lie on the sward in the shadow of green boughs, to
listen to the songs of summer, to drink in the sunlight, the air, the
flowers, the sky, the beauty of it all.*

RICHARD JEFFERIES

Watching wildlife is a relaxed occupation which can be enjoyed during those leisure hours after a busy day, following a period of intense activity, or at weekends and when on holiday. Today, many of us spend out lives in perpetual motion; it can be a great relief, therefore, to slow down and take note of the natural environment. The poet, W H Davies, recognized this when he wrote in his poem *Leisure*: 'What is this world if full of care we have no time to stand and stare.'

The following chapters give a taste of the fauna and flora that can be easily observed in a wide variety of habitats; it is not a definitive study, but rather more a personal collection.

If you choose to study one or two particular habitats, you will become increasingly intimate with the species that live there. On the other hand you may prefer to observe a variety of habitats, if so you will derive great pleasure from endless changes of wildlife that live there. Never underestimate the contribution made by weather and season, for a year in the natural world is ever-changing, with the plants and animals responding, each in their own particular way. Migrations, life cycles, growth and decline, will play their part in providing fresh and exciting aspects of wildlife, many of them quite unique to you as the observer. Watching wildlife costs little money, except perhaps the use of transport to get to where you are going, and most of your time you need no equipment, certainly not at first, although one or two items may come along with experience. The rewards, in purely

non-materialistic terms, are immeasurable, as you discover, like Jefferies, 'The new-mown hay is scented yet more sweetly in the evening – of a summer's eve it is always too soon to go home.'

Awaiting every one of us who enjoys a walk in the countryside, be it field or seashore, are countless intimate and wonderful moments of personal discovery. It is simply a matter of tuning-in to the environment; waiting, watching, listening, smelling and touching. Those neglected senses of ours have been over-exercised in the hubbub of the town. Your switchboard has been overloaded with cacophony, fidgeting and the advertising media-man's visual stimuli in a way which numbs, rather than sharpens your senses. But once you have heard 'the songs of summer' you will be ready to begin the exciting process of observation, ie, *looking to some purpose*. Try to project yourself into the situation by thinking about it and asking yourself questions. Slowly, observation will provide a few answers and then you may truly begin to experience the natural world about you.

That accord with nature is both a state of mind and a physical experience – a willingness to accept the creatures and plants that share the world with us; a willingness to understand that each in its own way is a perfect peak of its evolution, and a single mesh in the network of

OPPOSITE:
*There are seven small crabs hiding among these shells. Can
you find them? This is the sort of problem you may
encounter on the shore.*

life that enmeshes us all. All we need to do is to relax for as Jefferies said:

> It is only while in a dreamy, slumberous, half-mesmerised state that nature's ancient papyrus roll can be read – only when the mind is at rest, separated from care and labour; when the body is at ease, luxuriating in warmth and delicious langour; when the soul is in accord and sympathy with the sunlight, with the leaf, with the slender blades of grass, and can feel with the tiniest insect which climbs up them as up a mighty tree – the mind joys in the knowledge that it, too, is part of this wonder – akin to the ten thousand thousand creatures, akin to the very earth itself.

That pleasure, if you so desire, will be with you wherever you may go: in the confines of the city and town you will find new beauty; by the waterside fresh creatures to watch; on the high moors and down in the estuary, bird calls and silence; in a single tree more life than you dreamed possible; in scented field and colourful hedge a host of creatures among the jungle grasses; in quiet woodland the muted music of wind through the leaves with its rich background of bird song and where the waves tumble on to the shore the wild calls of the gulls and treasures from the narrow margins of the seas.

Spend a little while on safari in the grass jungles.

Winter grass entombed in ice.

ART AND OBSERVATION

Living within the Dartmoor National Park, Jayne Netley is always close to wildlife, but while she enjoys depicting moorland birds, she is equally happy capturing the colours of the drift line on a beach. Detail fascinates her. She simply *has* to include every shell, paint each delicate leaf, and record the intricate structure of flowers. The ladybird is her trade mark and she has painted this tiny, much-loved insect into many of her pictures.

Jayne Netley's ability to observe closely and then reproduce behavioural studies in line or colour is a happy gift; the resulting picture, however, is seldom created without preliminary sketches and notes. While drawing the cuckoo spit, the little frog hopper jumped on to her brush and sat there; the hermit crabs were not so obliging and constantly moved around; the blue tits were observed through her cottage window. So, with words and brush, we have tried to record nature as we see it. We hope our observations will help you to find the time to stop and really *look* at the natural environment. I am quite sure you will be amazed at its diversity, ingenuity and beauty.

Completed illustration of cricket and grasshopper.

9

Observing these small mammals takes infinite patience: harvest mouse (top left); field mouse (top right); bank vole (bottom left); common shrew (centre); field vole (bottom right).

AMONG THE SEA PINKS

The habits of animals will never be thoroughly known till they are
observed in detail. Nor is it sufficient to mark them with attention
now and then; they must be closely watched.

PHILIP HENRY GOSSE

In the early morning sunlight the calling of the gulls fills the air, their music as old as the cliffs that are their ancestral colony. Here countless generations of herring gulls have merged their lives with the sea in an unchanging seasonal rhythm that ensures their continuity. Colonies of herring gulls are common around the British coast. There is, therefore, ample opportunity to observe a bird which engages in so many behavioural activities. Few natural history pastimes can rival the pleasure of gull-watching during those sunny spring days of clear blue skies and balmy sea breezes.

The best time to start gull-watching is in early March. At this time of the year the gulls are typically observed sitting together on roof-tops, street lamps and other suitable vantage points. Differentiating between the sexes is easier when the birds are close together; the male is stockier in build, slightly more erect, seemingly more alert and generally more robust. Unlike many birds, adult herring gulls have no plumage-colour differences. For a week or more the pairs can be observed feeding, resting and flying together. Most herring gulls pair for life, but during the winter months they will separate to feed around the beaches within a few miles of their colony site. Then, with the onset of spring, they will be reunited.

On a sunny day, usually in March, all the gulls of a particular area gather together in the sky, wheeling and calling, before flying to the site of their colony. Here a few flight members may alight and stay awhile before the whole throng flies off again. The gulls are making a reconnaissance of their breeding site. A few days later there will be a mass arrival at the colony; now the birds can be observed during the ensuing weeks. When a pair arrives together at their chosen piece of territory, that wonderful, wild clarion call rings out as they proclaim their occupation. For the next few days they do very little except sit around, preen, sleep and fly off to feed. Then the courtship routine begins in earnest. Bonding between the pairs is cemented by ritualistic behaviour which has been triggered by a combination of warmth, light, season and natural bodily rhythms.

At about this time it is advisable to pick a pair and concentrate on watching them, perhaps visiting the site several times during the course of a week. You will notice that periodically over the next few days the female will court her partner as he stands firmly on their chosen spot. Round and round her male she walks and each time she comes near his front she pauses, and gently, almost beseechingly, she brushes his chest feathers with her caressing beak; as her head lifts upward she utters a plaintive mewing call, two flute-like notes. For a few days the male apparently ignores her. Sometimes they fly off to feed but they remain close together, as if joined by a string. Later, when they return to the breeding site, the performance is repeated. Her calling is reminiscent of the food-begging call of a young gull; eventually he succumbs and

Herring gull alighting to claim territory (top left); mating occurs several times before eggs are laid (top right); territory-holder stretches neck upwards as a signal to warn off an intruder (centre left); grass pulling is the next warning if a stubborn intruder refuses to fly off the territory (centre right); if both warning signals fail, a tussel ensues and the intruder is invariably driven off (bottom left).

Courtship (top); clarion call (left); wide-awake eyes and multi-purpose beak (right).

regurgitates an offering of partly digested fish which she eagerly accepts. Courtship continues with the male apparently ignoring the female's 'chest rubbing' and plaintive calls. One day, however, he gives in and replies to her call, raising his head alternately with hers. Shortly after this he will lead her to the spot he has chosen for the nest by leaning forward as he walks, mewing as she had done before. When he gets there, he rocks forwards on his legs and bobs his head up and down, while continuing to make a 'choking' call. Very quickly the female replies with a similar call and action; this behaviour indicates that they are in agreement over the choice of nest site. Because these particular behavioural patterns are frequently performed, it is not difficult to make your observations.

At the appointed time the male mounts the female and she repeats her courtship head-tossing routine by rubbing her bill on his chest. As they make contact he utters a very distinctive and hoarse call, his vocal sac swelling with the effort as her eggs are fertilized. In a colony of several hundred birds this mating call can be heard ringing out throughout the day; the same cry fills the air in seaside towns where gulls build their nests on roofs.

The next stage is nest building and this is a hectic time, for while herring gulls make a very poor nest in relation to other birds' efforts, they do work extremely hard. Grass, bracken and dead foliage are pulled out of the ground on the cliff-top and carried in the beak back to the nest site. Some gulls are more adept at collecting material than others, for while a few will carry a mass of vegetation thus causing them to fly blind, others go home with little more than a single stick. Unfortunately, the wind often blows the material away, but persistence pays off and eventually a passable nest is formed. Then, among the flowering sea pinks, up to three eggs are laid; the pair will take it in turns to incubate the eggs. The non-incubating bird will take the opportunity to feed; on very hot days the

Ledge nesters: guillemot (left); razorbill (right).

15

incubating bird is frequently seen with its beak wide open, an effective method of lowering body temperature.

From now on you will observe all sorts of territorial disputes. After all, the colony is a very crowded place and each pair is confined to a very small space. As in every community there are always the 'bully-boys' who have to 'try it on' or seek to interfere with others. So it is inevitable that an intruder will trespass on the pair's territory. When this happens ritual behaviour helps to settle the dispute. The guarding bird struts, with neck stretched high, towards the intruder and usually this forces the latter to fly off. If this strutting does not work, the defender walks up to a patch of grass, seizes some in its beak and pulls at it, straining every muscle. The sight of this ritual sends most intruders off, but there is always one prepared to be more persistent, so as a final warning the defender rushes forward and seizes the wing of the intruder and a fight ensues, but seldom is blood drawn. This

defensive behaviour avoids risking mayhem and slaughter by fierce and death-dealing battles – a fine example of how survival is ensured by ritual behaviour.

While all this is going on the three eggs will have hatched and the pair will be kept busy gathering food for the chicks. When they want food – and that seems to be every hour of the day – you will hear their plaintive calls as they beg for nourishment. Once again ritual behaviour comes to their aid as the chick pecks at the red spot on the adult's beak. As soon as one of the parents arrives back from the food-gathering trip the chick starts tapping that spot. Three or four taps is usually enough and the parent opens its beak and regurgitates a lump of food. For the first few days, small green shore crabs are the main diet, but it is not long before all manner of oddments are brought in and regurgitated in front of them.

A certain amount of cannibalism occurs at this time, especially if a chick strays out of its

Cliff-dwelling rabbits are expert climbers, but their young often fall prey to hunting great black-backed gulls.

territory, but the fully fledged survivors can be watched as they strengthen their wing muscles by short periods of wing flapping. It is at this stage in their life that unfortunate fledglings fall down the cliff, but most herring gulls succeed in raising two of their three chicks. First flight is a rather hit-and-miss affair, especially the landing, and it is often amusing to watch them trying to alight on a rocky spur.

By October adults and young will be seen on the shore, the young usually cajoling the adults with their begging call; this is a common spectacle on any beach around the coast and even in harbours at low tide. But very soon the adults leave the chicks to fend for themselves; the family will go its separate ways until the following spring when they return to the regular meeting place and so another season begins.

Herring gulls are a highly successful species, mainly because they are so adaptable and willing to take advantage of man's activities and his environment. It is man's activities that are driving the gulls away from their natural seashore habitats; man puts up promenades, where gulls once built their nests; seaside cafes and beach chalets drive them away from the dunes and beaches. So the gulls have begun to take over our roof-tops in lieu of lost cliff-sides. Herring gulls are great plunderers of our waste food; they know how to overcome the lids of litter baskets and when to fly in to the beach after the holiday-makers have gone home, and so find rich pickings in throw-away sandwich packs and chip packets; they follow the trawlers as the fishermen gut the catch. If you watch them at work hunting their food you will see them plunge-diving in the shallow water of harbours for dead fish; risking life and limb among bulldozers and fire on rubbish dumps; following the plough and getting back to the field early next morning to wait for the farmer if the job is not finished; or 'marking time' with their

Look for a sand martin's nest in soft cliffs.

feet on the sandy shore, to release small crabs, worms and shellfish. This behaviour is easily visible to the naked eye, but binoculars can prove an asset when some aspects of behaviour are out of range.

The herring gull is an ideal subject for the keen observer of behaviour, but other species which inhabit the cliffs are equally rewarding. Small groups of razorbills are often found on near-vertical cliffs, nesting in the cracks, usually among the large colonies of guillemots living on the narrow ledges – some of these ledges are so incredibly narrow one wonders how the birds find room to nest. But in the breeding season you will find them there in tightly packed rows: guillemots are very social birds.

One of the most breathtaking sights – and sounds – is to be experienced in a kittiwake colony, especially at the time when the bluebells are out on the cliff-tops. Try to visit a colony on a sunny morning, when the great beauty of the birds can be seen to best advantage. They nest on sheer cliffs and have become masters of the craft of nest-fixing. Using mud as the base material they pound it into a sticky mass with their feet, and because they 'glue' their nests in place in this way they are tempted to nest-build in unstable and

PORPOISE DAWN

It was a golden dawn to be remembered for the fresh sea air which was clean and alive with the calls of the kittiwakes, and the marvellous view from the cliff-top. A fulmar glided past, buoyant on the up-draught; on ledges beneath the bluebell slope guillemots crowded together conversing in their unbirdlike growling language. Then, amid the sea-calls of countless gulls, came a sharper, whistling note, faintly at first from around the small headland. It grew more distinct and then the sea below became alive with the arrival of a school of porpoise, fifteen to twenty gleaming black backs and bright white bellies arced up, over and down, keeping close together. As they drew nearer their shapes could be seen through the water, beautiful small whales, once so common around the coast.

Now they are threatened by chemical run-off from rivers, the build up of toxic substances in the food chain, and the accidental (all too common) drowning when entangled in fishermen's nylon monofilament nets. Threatened too by the incessant throb of power-boat propellers, sonar and seismic explosions that obscure their own delicate and sensitive sound communications. In the dawn light it was unthinkable that such lovely and sensitive animals might soon be yet another statistic in the catalogue of environmental disasters.

erupt into the air and wheel out from the cliff, filling the sky with their musical calls, uttering their name 'kittiwake, kittiwake'.

Each year in November the fulmars visit their nest site. They arrive suddenly, then sit on the water calling to each other, occasionally flying up to the nest site to survey the scene. Typically they disappear the following day, but periodically throughout December, January and February they will land on their nest ledges, perhaps finally settling in April. Here they remain until their departure late in September for the wide open stretches of the North Atlantic where they over-winter. (An excellent book by that late great ornithologist, James Fisher, is number six in the 'New Naturalist Series' called *The Fulmar*. It is published by Collins.) Have you ever watched a fulmar flying? They are true masters of the air and are able to glide indefinitely, using the updraughts against the cliffs to rise high and then plunge down with effortless ease tilting to right or left just enough to catch the smallest eddy, seemingly weightless.

When watching fulmars, or indeed any sea-bird, your spirits will soar with them: a herring gull hanging on the wind, cushioned on the upward surge of the sea breeze is a most ethereal sight; watch one gliding along the moving curve of a grey storm wave, inches above the foaming sea, and slipping away as the white crest gathers before tumbling into the roaring surf. Listen to the wild sea-calls of the sea-birds when the gales rush out of Siberia and send the storm waves crashing against the cliffs. And then again, in the spring of the year, find a hollow on the cliff-top where wind-pruned gorse diverts the breeze, and stay awhile to enjoy the music of the sea spirits and absorb the beauty of it all.

precipitous spots, often with disastrous results. They are scavengers, feeding on fish-waste thrown overboard from trawlers – I know of one colony that thrives largely on the raw sewage outfall. But do not let this put you off. Marvel at their dexterity as they suddenly

FIELD-WORK

Visit a herring-gull colony in the late spring or early summer and watch their behaviour –

courtship, mating, grass-pulling, brief fights and feeding rituals. Listen to their varied calls and notice how each is associated with a particular pattern of behaviour. Search along the tideline for the feeding signs of herring gulls: dismembered crabs and sea urchins and cracked-open shells. Search for clues by following their web-footed tracks on the beach or among the dunes.

Why not keep a diary of a year's events at a colony or on a known seashore? By recording their calls and adding your own commentary you will create a fascinating record of a year in the life of a colony.

Watch how gulls break open cockles by dropping them from high above a beach. Feed them with scraps and photograph them as they fly and hover. How many different species of gulls can you find? Try to recognize their different age/plumages or seasonal changes of plumage.

In winter keep watch on the sea from the promenade and cliffs. Look out for cormorants fishing, migrant ducks and any unusual sea-birds. Keep a look out for the arrival of fulmars if they nest in your area. Among flocks of gulls around the beaches always keep an eye open for the odd rarity, you never know what may turn up. Above all simply enjoy the gulls and their wild calls.

SITES TO VISIT

Wonderful cliff-top sites exist all around our coast and many sea-birds can be watched from coastal footpaths. The following suggested sites are among some of the best to observe behavioural patterns.

St Abb's Head

Visitor centre and ranger service. High sea cliffs 20km north of Berwick-upon-Tweed. Largest mainland sea-bird breeding site between Angus and Yorkshire. Nationally important populations of guillemots and kittiwakes, also shags, razorbills, fulmars and puffins.

Isle of May, north-east Fife

Sea-bird populations on 60m cliffs. Limited accommodation at the Bird Observatory. Information from 46 Crossgate, Cupar KY15 5HS. Tel Cupar (0334) 54038.

The Farne Islands, Northumberland

A National Trust nature reserve. Information from National Trust, 8 St Aidans, Seahouses, Northumberland NE68 7SR. Tel Seahouses (0665) 720651. Group of islands providing summer home for 17 seabird species including puffins, kittiwakes, eider ducks, guillemots, fulmars and terns. Seal colony. Boats from Seahouses to Inner Farne and Staple Island. Breeding season 15 May–15 July inclusive. Staple 10.30 am–1.30 pm; Inner Farne, 1.30 pm–5.00 pm. Out of season 1 April–14 May and 16 July to end September: both islands 10.00 am–6.00 pm.

Hermaness

Information: NCC Sub Regional Office, 73 Commercial Street, Lerwick, Shetland ZE1 0AB. Great and arctic skuas, puffins, gannets, guillemots and fulmar breeding. Grey and common seals.

Skomer

Information: NCC Plas Gogerddan, Aberystwyth, Dyfed SY23 3EB. Manx shearwater, storm petrels, fulmars, puffins, razorbills, guillemots and kittiwakes. Grey seals. Send to RSPB, The Lodge, Sandy, Bedfordshire for booket Reserves Visiting.

Berry Head Country Park, Brixham, Devon

Herring-gull colony, guillemots, fulmars, kittiwakes and razorbills.

ROCK HOPPIN'

Most curious and interesting animals are dwelling within a few yards of your feet, whose lovely forms and hues, exquisitely contrived structures, and amusing instincts, could not fail to attract and charm your attention.

PHILIP HENRY GOSSE

Our rich and varied coastline offers endless possibilities for exploration; from the wild regions of west Wales to the wave-cut platforms of south Devon; from the chalk cliffs of the south coast to the intriguing Isles of Scilly. In this section I will concentrate on rocky shores where the tumbled rocks and wave-cut platforms, often backed by startlingly beautiful cliffs, provide a habitat for an enormous variety of living animals. No other natural environment in the British Isles offers such a wealth of life as that which exists under rocks, in the rocks, behind the seaweed curtains and in the pools that abound there.

Twice every day the sea sweeps in and twice it ebbs to reveal the shining rocks and seaweeds. It is a harsh environment and the little animals that live there have adopted some fascinating strategies for survival. Think for a moment of some of the factors with which they have to contend: the drying effect of winds; the heat of summer sunshine and the ice-cold temperatures of winter; the ebb and flow of tides; the whole range of predators from fish to birds, and the intricate food webs that enmesh them all. While summer plenty may offer rich feeding, the titanic storms of winter present more formidable challenges.

Try to imagine, for a moment, what it must be like to live among those rocks when huge storm waves crash down with a force of tons to a square metre and hurl dustbin-sized rocks to and fro among a barrage of surf-spun pebbles and stones blasting everything with sand-saturated sea water. A testing environment, to say the least. But the creatures that live there survive and thrive in the very conditions that would mean annihilation to other forms of life. So you can see why I consider the creatures of the rock pools to be fairly special and certainly worth a close look. (Since you will be encountering a whole range of living creatures, many of which will be strange in shape, you need to take a good, simple field guide with you and the one I have found most useful is *Collins Pocket Guide to the Sea Shore* by John Barrett and C M Yonge. With over 750 illustrations, 280 of which are in superb colour, you will find most of your identification problems easily solved. In its twenty-seven years of publication, and with ten reprints, it is as fresh, practical and useful today as it ever was.)

And what forms of life are these great survivors? Plant-like sponges clothing the underside of rocks and beneath overhangs, flower-like sea anemones with stinging tentacles, sea squirts – small plastic-bag-like animals which squirt water when pressed – barnacles by the million cemented to the rocks, limy tubeworms looking like 3D hieroglyphics, flatworms, round worms, ribbon and bristle worms, sea cucumbers resembling semi-mobile gherkins, sea spiders, woodlice-like creatures, sandhoppers (perhaps we should call them rock-hoppers on the rocky shore), prawns, lobsters and crabs in stagger-

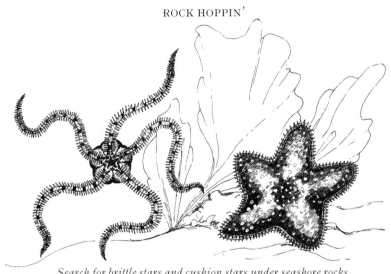

*Search for brittle stars and cushion stars under seashore rocks.
Always replace rocks after searching.*

ing variety. Shellfish of all shapes and sizes, sea urchins covered in sharp spines, starfish and brittle stars moving on tube-feet and fish from eel-like pipefish to slippery butterfish and endearing blenny. If you are very, very lucky you may come across cuttlefish, squid or octopus. Bottles are to be found – probably none with messages from shipwrecked mariners – and, unfortunately, broken glass, especially after summer beach barbecues, so always wear footwear when rock hoppin'. It is sensible to wear a warm sweater or anorak – it is surprising how the outer limit of the rocky shore is so much cooler and windier than the sheltered sunlit cliff-side.

WHERE AND HOW TO SEARCH

If possible choose a period of low spring tide – check the times in a local tide timetable which is usually available at a fishing tackle or marine sports shop. Spring tides occur at new and full moon and the sea ebbs its lowest about two to three days after the full and new moon date. Set off on your expedition a couple of hours before low water so that you follow the tide down, and since you will not be collecting – but only observing – you need take nothing but your hands. A net is more often a nuisance than an asset, although a

thermos flask and a picnic meal will probably be appreciated later in the expedition. On your way down to the sea's edge look more closely at the small narrow fissures in the rocks. Bend down and part the seaweed, it will probably be bladder-wrack, saw- or serrated-wrack, or knotted-wrack; look carefully in the cracks of the rock you have exposed and you might be lucky enough to discover some beadlet anemones. They look like half a small plum glistening with moisture for their tentacles will be withdrawn. Their survival techniques are simple for they are anchored firmly to the rock surface with a large sucker-disc, their body is soft and yielding to the onslaught of waves, and they retain moisture by hiding in damp gullies behind moist seaweed.

Behind one clump of seaweed you may well encounter a green shore crab. They vary in size from a small coin to the size of the palm of your hand, and their structure is quite beautiful. Two bright eyes on short stalks, two jointed feelers and, working like a pair of scissors, the mouth. Like all crabs they have ten legs, at least a perfect one has that number, but all too often you will find a crab with one, two or more legs missing, proof of the hazards of shore life. Eight of its legs are

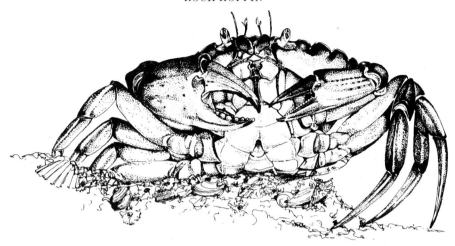

*New limbs for old. A four-year-old green shore crab with its
newly grown two-year-old nipper claw.*

used for walking and the front pair for offence, defence and for picking up or tearing pieces of food such as dead fish or shellfish. Frequently one of these large nipper claws is much smaller than the òther, this is probably because the crab lost one of its claws and is in the process of regrowing it.

Crabs grow by casting their entire 'shell', that is their hard outer skin, and in doing this they emerge through a space which opens up at the rear of their back. They pull themselves out, quite remarkably drawing eyes from eye covers, feelers from their jointed sheaths, legs from their armour-plated covering, until a soft flabby shiny crab lies beside its old shell. At such times they seek shelter for they are very vulnerable to attack. During the next couple of weeks their body grows and then slowly hardens again. It is during this growth period that limbs are replaced, growing from a tiny bud a little larger each time the skin is cast, which seems to be an annual event. A lucky crab, one which has avoided all predators, may live to an age of ten to fifteen years or even more, and measure 3in (8cm) across its back. Males and females mate throughout the year and crabs can be found with a clump of eggs attached to their underside in most months, although egg clumps are

most common between January and April in the south and October to May in the north. How many eggs? Well, as a conservative estimate, 190,000!

Another crab, admittedly less common on the shore but occasionally found near the lower limit of spring tides, is the large hermit crab. This fine fellow uses a whelk shell as a home, especially to protect the rear of his body which is not armour plated. Often attached to the whelk shell is an anemone which, although called the parasitic anemone, is not a parasite, as we shall discover in a moment. Also sharing this shell with the hermit crab is a ragworm which lives in the pointed end.

The reason for this three-way association becomes obvious when the crab feeds. The hermit crab, being highly mobile, covers a lot of ground thereby maximizing its chances of finding food. Having found sustenance, for instance a dead fish, it begins to tear pieces off and eat them. Deep inside the shell the ragworm scents the food and crawls towards the open end where the crab is feeding; it then creeps along the right cheek of the crab and actually takes pieces of the food from the crab's mouth.. While this appears to be a parasitic action, the constant movement of

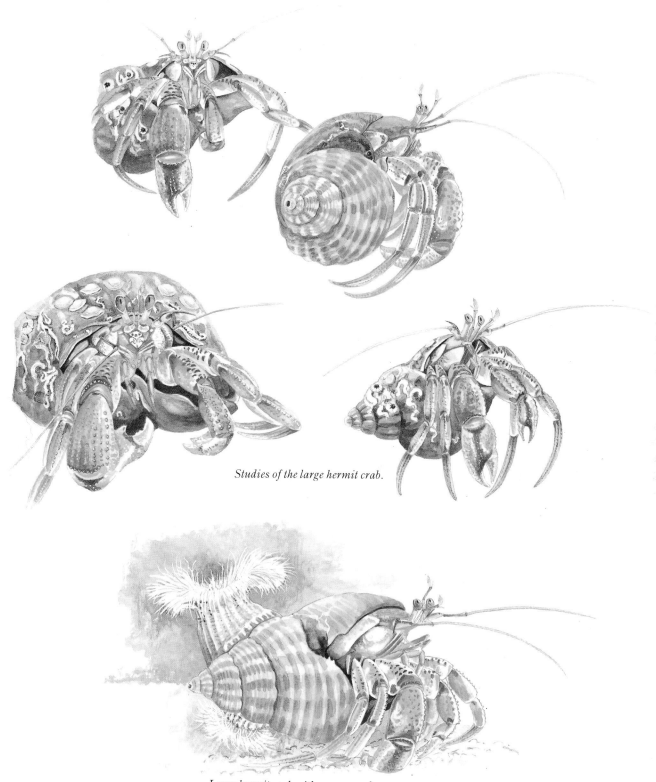

Studies of the large hermit crab.

Large hermit crab with commensal anemone.

the worm circulates water through the shell and helps rid it of the crab's waste products. So the ragworm is a sort of house cleaner. Meanwhile the open and spread poisonous tentacles of the anemone present a threat to any fish, a dogfish for example, that might decide the crab would make a good meal.

But the story does not end here, for the crab is an untidy feeder and it litters the seabed with pieces of its meal. Then when it walks on, the anemone bends over, trailing its tentacles over the sand, and like a vacuum cleaner picks up the pieces and so gets its share of the food. So it is that the three creatures, a hermit crab, ragworm and anemone, all live together in an old whelk shell. Such a symbiotic relationship is known as commensalism – 'feeding at the same table'.

While exploring the rocky shore, take a look under one of the seaweed-covered boulders, you will be amazed at the variety of life to be seen there. More crabs for instance, small flat, hairy ones with very flat nipper claws clinging tightly to the rock surface and known as broad-clawed porcelain crabs. If you see a reddish brown crab with clear blue joints scuttle away noisily into the shade of the upturned rock, that will be the fiddler or velvet swimming crab. It is the only crab that is likely to seize an unwary finger for it is fast and very fierce, especially as it rears back on its hind legs, snapping its business-like pincer claws like tiny castanets. It has a pair of bright red eyes which add to its ferocious appearance. Another noisy little fellow that flexes its tail end to flap into shelter is the squat lobster. Nearby may be some brittle stars – thin-armed starfish of varying colours from dark violet to red or white and with spots of colour on the disc and arms. Handle them *very* carefully, for they all too easily cast off one or more of their arms, hence the name brittle star. Here, too, will be our smallest starfish, almost pentagonal because its arms are so short, the cushion star.

As you look more intently at the rock you have turned over you become more and more aware of the large number of little animals that share its protection. Large patches of white tubeworms mingle with the fleshy mound of crumb-of-bread sponge, with openings at the summits of small prominences like the craters of miniature volcanoes, yellow, blood-red, scarlet and orange. Nearby may be the jelly-like spread of golden stars tunicate, a colonial sea squirt with an easily recognizable star-shaped pattern in a beautiful array of colours. They simply draw in sea water, which contains oxygen and suspended particles of possible food, strain into the gut and pass out the filtered sea water. These functions, not easily observed in so small a sea squirt, are much easier to see if you come upon a larger variety such as ascidella whose body can be up to three inches long and as thick as your thumb. Looking like a tiny pile of small pebbles and shell fragments is the dahlia anemone; when its tentacles are withdrawn is not immediately recognizable, although a large specimen when fully expanded may be as large as a small saucer. Its stout tentacles are adorned with a marvellous variety of colour patterns.

The delicate, spiny bodies of sea urchins grow up to 2in (5cm) across; they like to hide away under rocks. One, the purple-tipped sea urchin, often attaches itself to pieces of seaweed and shell fragments, an intriguing habit that would appear to be an unnecessary form of camouflage since it hides itself so well under rocks. But this behaviour serves some other, not yet deciphered purpose. As you become increasingly more familiar with the rocky shore, so you will discover new creatures and by observing them closely, you will learn about and enjoy the day-to-day activities of their secret lives.

Whenever you move a rock and turn it over, remember to replace it after you have observed the creatures it protects. However, always ensure that the urchins, starfish and other small creatures sheltering there will not be crushed.

FIELD-WORK

Sit and watch the sea-birds as they go about their daily lives and look for signs of their feeding. Watch a gull preening, it is a fascinating exercise in bird-head movement. Listen and try to recognize the varied bird calls.

Enjoy the colour, form and movements of the seaweeds and probe behind the wrack curtains for animals hiding from shore predators. Near low tide take a look under a large stone and watch how each individual animal moves. How is it adapted to survive in such a harsh environment? Take a really close look at some of these tiny creatures and you will be surprised by their infinite variety of form, design, colour and shape.

Use a shell as an improvised aquarium and create a temporary home for a brittle star, a porcelain crab or hermit crab. Keep still and watch what they do. Take a closer look at those tiny, white spiral limestone tubes of the coiled tubeworm on the fronds of the sea wracks. You might be surprised to discover one species spirals anticlockwise while the other adopts a clockwise movement.

If you have plenty of time, put some corallina seaweed into a shallow container of sea water and wait awhile: you will be amazed by the number of different animals that emerge from the plant. In the spring and early summer search for sea hares and the grey sea slug. The eggs of a great variety of animals can also be studied at this time of year.

SITES TO VISIT

Rocky shores are common all around our coastline and you should not have to travel far to find a suitable location. Look for areas of tumbled rocks and rocky platforms at the base of cliffs; if possible choose an area with plenty of good seaweed cover, as this offers

A LITTLE BROWN BIRD

There is a little brown bird which lives in a rocky cove nearby, that invariably appears when I visit the shore. It always sees me before I see it, and restlessly flutters ahead to alight on a wrack-covered rock. It is a rock pipit, a delightful little bird about the size of a sparrow but much slimmer. Nervous of intruders, it has lived in the cove for some years, maintaining its territory throughout the winter. Then with the arrival of spring it begins its gentle courtship, rising from a rock and uttering its trilling song, before settling once more. The pair nests among the tumbled rocks at the base of the cliff, midway between land and the sea where the orange lichens encrust and brighten the red sandstone. There is food in abundance on the shore. The rock pipit will run over the bladder-wrack or pause to probe beneath its fronds for sandhoppers and small worms; sometimes it is reflected in rock pools, or will join other birds pecking daintily among the high-tide flotsam for insects and their larvae, and the seeds that fall from the rich cliff-side flora. It feeds too among the noisy, predatory gulls – a tiny wind-blown tuft of seaweed at the very edge of the surf. In winter it defies the force-six gales, jinking through the spume-mist and in summer its delightful dancing flight above the sparkling sand is a joy to behold. Its presence enhances the quiet beauty of the cove; the rock pipit's frail form surviving in what, for so small a bird, must surely be a very hostile environment.

shelter for all the creatures that live there. It is most important to check a tide timetable and to follow the tide as it ebbs. Beware the rising tide in an unfamiliar place, it can so easily cut off your homeward route.

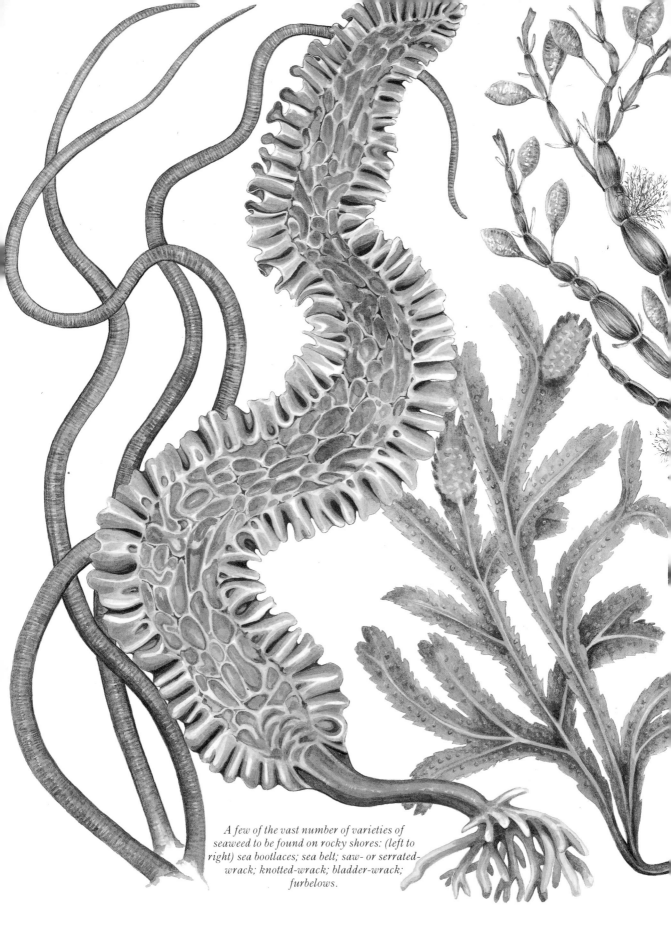

A few of the vast number of varieties of seaweed to be found on rocky shores: (left to right) sea bootlaces; sea belt; saw- or serrated-wrack; knotted-wrack; bladder-wrack; furbelows.

CRYSTAL POOLS

*A pretty tidepool, full of pure sea water, quite still, and as clear as
crystal. . . . from the rocky margin and sides the puckered fronds of
the Sweet Oar-weed sprang out, and gently drooping, like ferns
from a wall.*

PHILIP HENRY GOSSE (1852)

Tide pools of all shapes and sizes are waiting to be explored on the rocky shore around the coastline. They are home and shelter for a rich variety of life. As the tide ebbs, one by one they are uncovered from near high water mark to the extremity of low spring tide. To see what lives in these small rock basins one has to approach slowly and quietly and then wait at the edge: the creatures that live in tide pools are extremely wary and flee for cover at the slightest sign of danger.

One slow-moving animal, sometimes finding a temporary home in pools, is the common starfish. It is an active predator of shellfish, especially bivalves like mussels, oysters and scallop-type shellfish, which it seeks out with amazing determination. If you find one, pick it up and examine its underside. The first things you will notice are the rhythmically moving semi-transparent feet, each one terminating in a tiny sucker. One cannot fail to be impressed by the fact that they co-ordinate the movement of all their feet without the benefit of a brain.

It is an extraordinary ability and, in simple terms, it works as follows: in the centre, the junction point for its arms, is its mouth and surrounding it a nerve ring from which nerves branch out down the arms. These nerves stimulate areas of its body and so co-ordinate movement. While human beings, even with the benefit of a massive brain, sometimes trip over obstacles, the brainless starfish manages to co-ordinate all its feet to move smoothly in one direction. Watching it move, one cannot but be amazed at the beautiful motion, rhythmic and precise, almost balletic in quality. This 'walking' of innumerable tube feet is yet another marvel of the starfish – a living water-pressure system! The scientific explanation lies in another ring around the mouth. This one is a tube which has a series of branch tubes running along the arms and connected to them are hundreds of tiny 'bladders' to which the tube feet are joined. When the starfish gets the urge to move, water is drawn from the sea into the ring tube and forced along to these 'bladders' which expand and so force the tube foot to lengthen. The nerve network then gets to work and sends the impulse that causes all those feet to move in the required direction. Suction tips fasten on to a firm surface and the little creature glides away.

However scientific an explanation of behaviour may be, one is forever confronted with the wonder of its perfect beauty, and this so-called 'simple' animal has a living structure so delicately formed that we can only marvel at its 'rightness' for its way of life. Perfect co-ordination, a term that slips so easily off the tongue and which we admire in Olympic athletes, ballet dancers, acrobats and jugglers, is demonstrated by one of this earth's 'lower' forms of life.

When attacking a shellfish, the starfish creeps slowly up and over its shell. In the case of a mussel there is no escape for it is firmly anchored to the rock, but queen shells and scallops can jet propel themselves out of danger with astonishing speed. Once over the mussel the starfish exerts a steady pull and since it has all the time in the world, eventually the shellfish muscles tire and the twin valves gape open a little. An opening less than half a centimetre wide is all that is needed for the starfish to extrude its stomach through the gap and so digest the mussel. When fully fed it simply withdraws its stomach which then slips back within the starfish leaving only an empty shell to testify to a meal.

But the wonders of a starfish do not end there, for you may well discover one with, for example, four normal arms and one very short one – not the usual 'five-fingers' as named by fishermen. This one has obviously lost an arm, perhaps in an accident in a rough sea when a rolling stone trapped it. Nature makes escape possible, for starfish are able to cast off a trapped or injured arm and grow another one.

Occasionally the discarded arm grows four more!

Starfish are a pest among oyster beds and before the 'five-fingers' secrets were revealed, fishermen used to catch them by trailing bundles of ropes' ends over the beds. They then chopped them into small pieces and threw them overboard, confident that they were eliminating a pest. Unfortunately, due to the starfish's capacity for regeneration, the fishermen were to a limited degree extending the starfish population on their oyster beds.

A common crustacean is the prawn, and you will find them either clinging to seaweed or walking daintily over the pool bed. If you move, it will flip backwards and disappear into the seaweed curtains. It is a good idea to take a piece of fish (fish fingers with the brown crust removed will do nicely) along with you, tempt the prawn with a morsel and watch how it feeds. If two prawns seize it at the same time you will see plenty of action. Prawns grow by

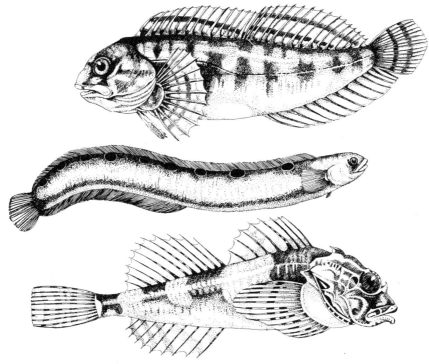

Small fish that you may discover behind the seaweed curtains of a pool:
blenny (top); butterfish (centre); long-spined sea scorpion (below).

casting their entire shell; their ghost-like skins can sometimes be found if you search carefully among the stones and shells on the pool bottom. After casting, their bodies harden quite quickly and a prawn is able to eat within a few hours of leaving its old skin.

Anemones are common on the rocky shores. These flower-like animals, spread their venomous tentacles like petals. On most southwestern beaches the greenish, snakelocks anemones, sometimes with pink-tipped tentacles, possess stinging cells which anaesthetize prey with which it comes into contact. Avoid bringing delicate skin into contact with anemone tentacles because the poison they emit can cause an unpleasant 'nettle-rash'. But there is no need to touch them to see them feed, simply drop a piece of fish in their vicinity and you can watch them slowly engulf and swallow it through the mouth in the centre of the tentacles. Dahlia anemones display wonderful patterns of grey, pale crimson, mauve and white, but they are a rather retiring species favouring the shade beneath rock overhangs and behind seaweed. If you enjoy painting, they provide a marvellous subject. I once found a dahlia anemone with a spread disc the size of a teaplate. The daisy anemone pushes its column into rock crevices and spreads its grey and brown tentacles over the sand. If you find a white, orange or brown anemone, and if it is open with its feathery mass of tentacles spread, it may well be a plumrose anemone. But all too often this anemone remains contracted as a small, raised mound, tight against the rock.

Many different fish can be found in rock pools but all are fast movers with exceedingly sharp eyes and they usually see you before you see them. But your patience will be rewarded with the sight of a timorous head peeping out from behind a seaweed frond, and then another, perhaps darting for the shade cast by a small rock. The blenny or shanny is a delightful little fish with big white lips and prominent eyes. In the spring the males turn almost black as they guard the rock holes where the female has laid her eggs. By dropping pieces of fish close to the pool's edge you can often persuade the blennies to come out and feed. In shallow sandy pools the smallest of our gobies is everywhere abundant, making sudden darting rushes that reveal its presence. This will be the common or sand goby, a master of camouflage, the colours of its body perfectly matching the sand on·which it comes to rest. Darting with breathtaking speed to engulf prey (or proffered fish) are either of the two common sea scorpion fish to be found in rock

ROCK POOL

Multi-coloured seaweed curtains drape its sides softening the textured shell-gravel bed where crabs and prawns live out their lives. Winter sanderlings, flighting in from the Arctic tundra, rest awhile beside it; limpets graze on each spring's crop of algae; in summer as the sea hares spawn their pink ribbons, the sea thrift cradling a herring gull's nest on the cliff-side sheds its petals on to its waters. Seven oystercatchers visit daily to feast on the mussels bordering its coralline rim.

Through untold centuries the tides have ebbed and flowed, instilling their rhythms into this pool's life and man has passed by as hunter and watcher. Yet despite the scientific technology that has taken him to the moon, he is largely ignorant of the subtle life forces at his feet – the intricate relationships and delicate networks that enmesh the life of this small pool. By day it holds the sun's revealing gleam; by night it captures the moon to illuminate secrets beyond our understanding, for we are but an infinitesimal part of the life-flow within and around this small rock pool.

Starfish studies.

Preparing to feed.

Starfish in feeding position.

Starfish regrowing two new arms.

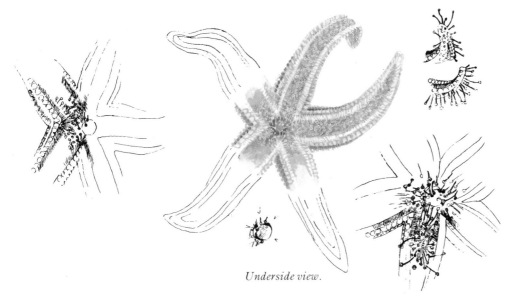

Underside view.

pools. The bullhead or father-lasher and the long-spined sea scorpion are easily recognized by their large, flattened and spined heads with bodies tapering away to the tail. Their mouths are comparatively large, well designed to seize live prey. Incapable of stalking, they lie in wait behind cover ready to rush out and swallow. They can be lured out by dropping pieces of fish into the water. However, not every pool harbours every species, but with a little experience you will learn what to expect in a particular kind of pool.

Signs of pollution are not uncommon on the seashore and quite recently some patient research by marine biologists revealed a poisonous substance that was wreaking havoc among the dog whelk populations. These small shellfish live and feed in rock pools, rocky shores and anywhere where there are mussels and barnacles on which to settle and launch their attack. They have a long ribbon-like tongue armed with sharp teeth. Slowly these bore a hole through the shell of a mussel, aided by an acid which softens it. It then inserts its proboscis and feeds. An ingenious, if uncommon feeding method.

At breeding time dog whelks gather together in rock crevices to pair before laying their eggs; at such times, in the winter, I have counted over forty whelks in a cluster. These creatures lay large masses of grain-sized eggs, up to as many as three hundred being laid by a single dog whelk. However, it would now be more correct to say 'they *used* to lay', for in recent years they have been stricken by a man-made disaster.

To rid the hulls of pleasure craft from fouling organisms such as barnacles and seaweeds, boat owners apply a coat of anti-foul before launching their craft each season. Recently, TBT, a highly effective anti-foul, became commercially available. Alas, it proved to be so effective that one part in many million parts of sea water proved to be highly toxic to certain shellfish. And the unfortunate dog whelk was the victim. All around our coasts during recent winters, not a single dog whelk egg was to be found – the entire population stopped laying eggs. Biologists set to work and discovered that TBT from the hulls of comparatively few boats had so polluted the sea with minute quantities of the new anti-foul that it spread throughout the shore line and caused what amounted to a sex-change within the dog whelk population, thus preventing the creatures from laying their eggs. Fortunately the substance is now banned, but while it was in use it provided a staggering example of how man can affect the environment.

FIELD-WORK

Check a tide timetable (you do not want to be cut off by a rising tide), follow the ebb tide down and explore the pools. Patience, silence and stillness will reveal many of the inhabitants, especially if you drop a few pieces of fish into the pool. Leave it for a while and visit

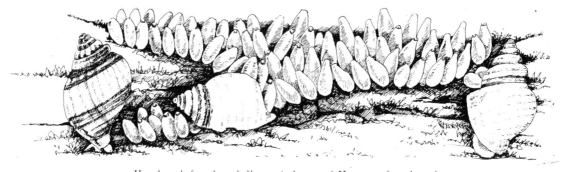

How long before dog whelks again lay eggs? Have you found any?

KEY TO PAGES 34–35
After the storm, the tideline:
1 rednose cockle; 2 thin tellin;
3 dogfish egg capsule; 4 slipper
limpet; 5 razor shell; 6 otter shell;
7 common whelk; 8 sea-snail shell;
9 cuttlefish 'bone'; 10 barnacles;
11 oyster; 12 sting winkle; 13 netted
dog whelk; 14 tiger scallop;
15 auger shell; 16 rayed trough
shell; 17 painted top shell;
18 skate's egg capsule.

other pools before returning to watch the creatures that have come out to feed.

Try a night visit to the pools. Use a torch or Tilley lamp. There will be much more to see than in daylight, for the creatures in rock pools come out at night and go about their business undisturbed by predators.

Feed the anemones and prawns and watch how they behave. Use a good field guide (see 'Further Reading') to identify a few of the seaweeds and animals you are watching. In autumn and winter search for the eggs of dog whelks to ascertain if a few survivors from TBT are rebuilding the population. Find a starfish, examine it closely, replace it in the water upside down and watch it slowly somersault into its natural position, revealing all its tube feet as it does so.

Enjoy the scents, sounds and colours of sea-moved seaweeds; contemplate the complete environment as you watch and wait beside a rock pool. It can be really rewarding.

SITES TO VISIT

The coast is never far from most parts of the British Isles, but if you are looking specifically for rock pools choose a place where the ebb tide reveals a long rocky platform. Most seaside resorts have 'Information Centres' and if you call in or send for brochures, you can usually locate good spots – although they do tend to emphasize the sandy beaches. Ordnance Survey maps reveal cliff areas with paths down to secluded coves where you can explore and discover so much about the natural history of the habitat.

ALONG THE BEACH

*Few, very few, are at all aware of the many strange, beautiful or
wondrous objects that are to be found by searching on those shores
that every season are crowded by idle pleasure seekers.*

PHILIP HENRY GOSSE (c1852)

At first glance a sandy beach looks an unlikely place to find sea life, with its flat clear surface constantly swept by the ebb and flow of tides and pounded by surf and storm waves. Yet on many of our sandy beaches live a great variety of animals which, because of the harsh conditions, have adapted to living in the sand. It is literally 'the life under the beach deckchairs' for as you walk along the edge of the low tide you may well be passing over thousands of small life forms safely buried in their sandy burrows. The vast majority are shells, but crabs, starfish and sea urchins live there too. But first, how do we find them?

SEARCHING FOR SIGNS

Look carefully along the upper shore tide-line and the surrounding areas of sand for any scattered shells. Many of these will have been living a little lower down. After this initial sortie walk along the sea's edge and look for signs in the sand: holes and small depressions of varying shapes and sizes. These usually provide clues to what is living below and digging carefully with a spade will often reveal the animal. Other signs are left by the gulls: the torn-apart shell of a crab, the split test of a sea urchin and opened shells, usually bivalves, that have provided a meal for a feeding gull. Lastly, watch for movement in damp sand and small pools: the occasional shrimp burying in, the dart and rush of a small goby, the camouflaged form of small flatfish or the flash of silver as a sand eel dives head first into the sand and disappears from sight.

SECRETS OF THE SANDS

Most of the shell-life living in the sand is composed of bivalves and in order to take in the life-giving sea water they extend long tubes called syphons up to the surface; one tube to take water and its suspended food in, the other to pass it out after the food and oxygen have been extracted. It is these syphons that leave the holes and depressions on the surface. Often you will see a jet of water shoot into the air as you walk along as the pressure of your foot disturbs a razor shell. Large examples may be up to 10in (26cm) long and their burrowing rate is phenomenal as they can shoot down 2ft 6in (75cm) in four or five seconds, and digging them up from that depth can be very hard work.

Far less active is a large bivalve, almost the size of your hand, called the otter shell. Its syphons are as big around as a finger and the shellfish lives some 18in (45cm) or more below the surface. Then there is a wealth of smaller shells for you to discover: the delicate, thin tellin in shades of pink, orange and white; the faroe sunset shell blazoned with rays like a setting sun; multi-hued, banded wedge shells and the snail-like natica. This latter is a hungry predator of shellfish. It bulldozes its way through the sand in search of prey, which it envelops in its huge prehensile flat foot before making a neat round hole through which it pushes its long proboscis to feed. Assisted by acid, the boring is made by a special boring organ on its body. If you search among the empty shells on the beach you will notice that some of them have neat 1mm holes – a sure sign that natica has been feeding.

In the small shallow pools among the tide-formed furrows, pause and wait, for there you may see some flatfish, about 2cm in diameter: baby plaice, flounders, turbot and sole. The best way to find them is to riffle your extended fingers through the sand, watching out for movement, and if you are fortunate you will see one swim a short distance before settling in a tiny cloud of sand grains that quickly re-camouflage it. In such small pools there will be the ubiquitous shrimp, not easily seen until you disturb it but then you will have an ideal opportunity to watch how it buries itself. First you see it makes a rapid shuffling movement with its legs, at the same time its swimming 'flaps' go into motion pushing the disturbed sand backwards, forming a shallow trough beneath its body. Then it raises and lowers side-flaps on its body which push the sand into a bank along its side. Relaxing into its trench, its feelers sweep sand backwards over its body, thus adding to the camouflage of its sand-coloured form.

Common on many of our beaches is the lugworm which local fishermen call Harry Nicola (I suspect an unintended pun on its hermaphrodite habits). It lives in a U-shaped burrow lined with mucus from its body. On the surface the sandy worm-like cast is formed as the worm burrows, literally eating its way through the sand and absorbing the fragments of food before excreting the cleaned sand, rather as squeezing a toothpaste tube produces a line of paste. A few centimetres away is a shallow depression formed as the worm draws down water in order to breathe. The worm itself may be up to 15in (20cm) or more below the surface – hence bait digging is such hard work.

Another worm you will encounter on some beaches, is the sand mason worm. Its protective covering of sand grains can be seen as a pencil-like tube extending about 1in (2.5cm)

above the surface and surmounted by a number of branches so that it resembles a tiny tree. The worm itself, some 10in (25cm) long, will be safely hidden perhaps 2ft (60cm) deeper down. It constructs this tube by collecting fragments of shell and minute stones by using a mass of tentacles which project out from its head. With these it draws the building material in, places it where required and then secures it with a glue-like mucus from glands in its body. Not a bad effort for a 'mere worm'. Look for remains of these tubes on the tide-line and examine them with a × 10 hand lens. Their structure is amazing and many of the particles, when magnified, can easily be recognized as parts of shells.

As well as the obvious signs of worms, star-shaped depressions indicate where a sea urchin, the sea potato, is buried. It has modified spines on its underside shaped like paddles and it uses these to push aside the sand as it slowly sinks down to safety. If you find one of these urchin holes, dig down to about 4in (10cm) below the surface and you will come across the little creature. Place it on the sand and watch it as it reburies, or hold it in your hand before doing so and observe the movement of the spines.

There is much, much more to be discovered as the ebb tide uncovers the sand and each fresh visit you make and each new beach you explore will reveal something new. Best of all perhaps, you will find new enjoyment in what may be a familiar setting.

AFTER THE STORM

In autumn and winter, and even occasionally during the summer, a storm blows up and sends the surf pounding on to the shore. A few days later as the waves subside a long line of flotsam and jetsam can be seen along the high-tide line. This is a great place to explore, for the storm strands all kinds of rare treasures for the naturalist and shore watcher. Most abundant of all will be seaweed of all kinds,

most of it torn from the rocks and piled in long windrows, but among it will lie a rich harvest of interest.

Many of the shells discussed at the beginning of the section will be found here; periodically a particularly fierce storm coinciding with spring tides will bulldoze out a vast mass of shell-life. I have seen rednose cockles lying, in places 2ft (60cm) deep, over an area the size of a bowling-green. Among them an occasional cockle writhed and turned as its red foot sought foothold before somersaulting the shell towards the sea; grey and white otter shells, smashed against the sea wall by the force of the waves, and countless shells of many kinds gaping in the cold blizzard conditions that slowly drew life from their delicate bodies. It all seemed a tragic, sad waste of life, yet perhaps it was a natural way to control populations, for in subsequent years the same scene of destruction will be repeated.

Lying among the seaweed you may find some mermaid's purses, the egg cases of dogfish and skate. Most will be empty, but an odd one here and there may still harbour its embryo, a tiny developing fish attached by

blood vessels to a yolk sac about the size of a chicken's egg. The baby fish takes from five to seven months to grow within the horny case. Here too will be the white masses of whelk egg capsules. Pick them up and look closely and in some of the capsules you will see a dozen or so baby whelks, partly formed. Such egg masses can be as large as a melon and have been formed by several whelks depositing their capsules together. You will almost certainly find cuttlefish 'bones'. These are the internal shells of cuttlefish, often used to feed budgies, and today, unfortunately, such finds are frequently tainted with tar and oil.

Sometimes a large balk of timber will be covered with goose barnacles. In medieval times these barnacles, which bear only a passing resemblance to geese, were believed to grow on trees and turn into geese. They do perhaps provide an example of how continuing observation and experiment reveals secrets of wildlife. It was John Vaughan Thompson, an army surgeon who delighted in marine study, who finally exploded the myth. By careful study and observation he discovered the barnacle's early stages and re-

KEY TO PAGES 38–39
1 herring gull and juvenile; 2 lesser black-backed gull; 3 common gull; 4 black-headed gull (summer), winter plumage (inset).

INSET:
1 lesser black-backed gull chick and egg; 2 common gull chick and egg; 3 herring gull chick and egg; 4 black-headed gull chick and egg.

vealed its true life history. Goose barnacles settle out of the plankton on to any floating object and have been found on bottles, tins and once on an electric light bulb attached to its brass collar.

SEA-BIRD WATCHING

This great abundance of available food draws in vast numbers of gulls and this in turn provides an exceptionally good opportunity for gull watching. On many promenades this can easily be done from a parked car. A small pair of binoculars will allow quite detailed study of the birds.

Herring gulls and black-headed gulls (these birds only have 'black' heads in the summer) will probably be the most numerous, but lesser and great black-backs, common gulls and the occasional little gull will all come in to feed. Running along the edge of the tide you will see small parties of turnstones busy flicking over seaweed in search of small crustaceans. It is a vibrant, excited scene, full of flying, feeding, squabbling, calling sea-birds, a mêlée of wildlife sufficient to satisfy any observer with a little time to spare.

FIELD-WORK

In summer search for signs of life under the sand and spend a little time beside the tiny sandpools. Paddle along the tide's edge on the lookout for all the surprises the sea may offer. Take a torch or Tilley lamp and go down after dark – as long as it is low tide – and see some of the small creatures that keep themselves out of sight when daylight hunters like the gulls are on duty. In the quietness enjoy the moon-path and the play of lights on the water and the shadows and highlights of sand furrows and pools. Listen awhile to the soft sea sounds, the murmur of wavelets caressing the beach and the far-away call of oystercatchers.

You do not need to know anything about the shore (except to watch for rising tides) to enjoy it, for exploration and discovery brings its own pleasures. *Collins Field Guide to the Seashore* and Collins 'New Naturalist Series': *The Seashore* will answer all your queries when you return home.

In winter watch the sea-birds living their lives, especially feeding, and try to identify what they are eating. Explore the tide-line for flotsam and jetsam treasures. If there is a gale

Turnstones can be watched from most seaside promenades.

blowing, walk the winter beach and thrill to the roar of the surf.

SITES TO VISIT

Torbay
Torbay in south Devon has a wonderful range of beaches, teeming with life. Information: Paignton Tourist Information Centre, The Esplanade, Paignton TQ4 6ED. Tel: **558383**.

Rye Harbour, Sussex
Warden, 1 Coastguard Cottages, Rye Harbour, Sussex. Shingle flora and sea-bird colonies. Information Centre open April to September; October–March weekends and Wednesdays.

Dungeness, Kent
Information: Warden, Boulderwall Farm, Dungeness Road, Lydd, Romney Marsh TN29 9PN.
Botany, butterflies and birds. Ideal beach for sea-watching.

Slapton Sands, South Devon
Long shingle beach. Beautiful beach flora.

With so many miles of coastline the variety of beaches available will offer you endless enjoyment. Every beach is different, and the local Ordnance Survey maps will reveal some of those quiet, out-of-the-way places. There you may find seals, basking sharks cruising by, huge stranded jellyfish and frenetic sea-bird colonies.

FEATHERED FLOTSAM

At first I thought it was a cormorant. It lay in a bedraggled heap on the windrow of storm-stranded seaweed, flung ashore with all the flotsam and jetsam that forms the modern plastic tide-line. A frayed trawl-line snaked across its large webbed feet and near its head a lump of whelk egg capsules vibrated in the gale. But this was no cormorant, rather a once-white gannet, now shiny with the clinging filth of oil smothering every feather. I tried to imagine how it had happened. Perhaps one sunny morning it had been flying with others high over a shoal of mackerel. It had dived with that breathtaking accuracy that captures a specific fish and surfaced under the edge of an oil slick. There was no escape – only the long painful days of trying to clean off the oil with its beak and the searing burn of swallowed oil; blown by the storm wind into the surf to be smashed insensible and cast ashore. A solitary, oil-covered gannet, a sad, disturbing, mute testimony to man's uncaring pollution of the seas.

Alas! The modern plastic tideline.

OVER THE DUNES

If I cast into one side of the balance all that I have learned from the
books of the library and into the other everything that I have
gleaned from 'the books in the running brooks', how surely would
the latter turn the scales.

KONRAD LORENZ: *King Solomon's Ring*

With skylark song as an accompaniment to the flying gulls and the soft sound of the sea in the background, there is a welcome waiting on the dunes if one opts for a walk in the spring sunshine. It is a pleasure just to be there and to enjoy the shadowed wind sculptures on the dune slopes and in the slacks, for dunes are ever-changing, never two days alike as the sands move and re-form into fresh patterns.

The amazing thing about dunes is their mobility – thousands of tons of wind-blown sand creeping slowly inland as the seas give up their buried burden of eroded cliffs and under-water rocks. On a windy day watch the dry sand grains driving like a desert sandstorm over the surface of the beach. Watch how a stranded piece of wood is slowly buried; observe the sand rushing up the slopes of the foredunes (those nearest the sea) to the mo-bile, moving crests where the marram grass captures the sand in its barrier of stiff leaves and anchors it down with a network of underground stems and roots. If you move the sand away from the base of the plant you will see this network more plainly. On some dunes lyme grass grows as prolifically as marram but, with its grey foliage, is quite distinctive. In this environment every plant has a real struggle for survival, beginning on the drift line of the beach. Here grows the stiff prickly leaved saltwort lying among the dry seaweed, sea rocket with its lilac-coloured summer flowers, and several species of orache all of which have seeds spread by the sea. They are

surviving at the very edge of the land and rough surf sometimes washes over them.

As you search for the dune flowers, move inland away from the sea and you will begin to see how different plants cope with the extra-ordinary conditions found here. So, moving up from the strand-line to the marram-crested foredunes you will find the magnificent spiny sea holly, its bluish-green leaves marked with white veins and in July and August its powder-blue and mauve flowers are quite delightful. It survives here by sending a tap root as far down as 8ft (2.5m) and as it becomes buried by moving sand it responds by quick upward growth. Growing beside it may well be another plant with a different survival tactic – sea bindweed, which lies prostrate on the moving sand and probes into it with creeping undersand stems.

Farther inland dunes will be stabilized and support a rich variety of flowers. Most obvi-ous, but local, are the yellow blooms of evening primrose and the distinctive burnet rose. If you search carefully, and this is where careful observation pays dividends, you might come across twayblade orchids and frog orchids. Enjoy them where they grow and do not pick them. Finally, most distant from the sea, the sea buckthorn grows and displays its silvery leaves and orange berries in season.

From an observer's point of view one of the minor snags of a dune system is the number of people that go there. Often after a hot summer's day the sand is covered by human

43

*Signatures in
the sand:
1 snake;
2 rabbit;
3 natterjack
toad;
4 oystercatcher;
5 wind-etched
circles described
by marram
stems.*

footprints and all signs of wildlife have been obliterated. In order to avoid people, dunes are best explored early in the morning, after a still night following a windy day or in cold winter weather.

Animals of all kinds leave their own individual signatures. To start reading these signatures it is helpful if you begin to recognize a few of the common species. Gull prints, typically webbed, the large ones usually those of the herring gull and the smaller ones black-headed gulls, are usually in evidence. Always remain alert to what is flying overhead or moving about on the beach.

An intriguing signature you will certainly see if you search carefully are the arcs and circles cut into the sand by the down-pointed tips of marram grass. Even a small plant with perhaps a single leaf bent over, describes a perfect circle when blown by the wind.

At the edge of the dunes you may well find the tell-tale signs of herring-gull feeding: large

footprints, rather jumbled around the dis-membered and cleaned-out body of a crab. The reason it fed some distance from where it caught the crab is often because of distur-bance from other gulls, causing it to fly off to feed in peace. Oystercatchers leave a distinc-tive three-toed print and if you follow a line where one of these birds has walked you will see some neat holes punched into the sand between the footprints. These are made when the bird plunges its beak into the sand to retrieve and eat a sandhopper. Such signs are usually along the sand where the dunes begin, often quite close to the high-tide mark and not infrequently between patches of stranded seaweed.

Sand dunes are a favoured nesting place for shelduck. They often choose an old rabbit burrow during March and April in which to lay a dozen or more eggs. When the time comes to introduce their brood to the outer world, both parents accompany them down to the sea. The resulting line of tracks, although interesting in itself, hardly compares with the sight of the family evacuation. You will have to choose quiet dunes or a nature reserve to view this charming scene for, like most birds, they do not relish too much disturbance.

Where the dunes are stabilized and overgrown with grass, blackberry thickets and clumps of creeping willow will thrive; all this cover provides food and sanctuary for rabbits, hedgehogs, foxes, rats and mice, and

ABOVE:
Shelduck youngsters take a first walk down to the sea.

OPPOSITE:
Top to bottom, flowers that successfully colonize the moving sand of the dunes: yellow horned poppy; sea holly; sea bindweed.

tracks of these mammals are often found after a careful search. From their tracks the various animals living in a dune area may be identified, even if you do not see the animal itself. The place where they are living – or hiding – can sometimes be pinpointed by following a line of footprints; rabbit and fox holes actually occupied can be deduced from footprints entering or leaving, especially if the tracks are well marked and obviously fresh. If you come upon some fox tracks, follow them because nocturnal hunting foxes often attack and kill roosting birds, especially gulls that tend to roost in such areas. It will not be difficult to recognize the kill, either from remains or feathers close to the spot.

I have frequently followed rabbit tracks right down to the sea's edge, which even on a neap tide may be a hundred metres from the dunes. Why they go down to the sea remains a mystery, but I have observed the tracks quite frequently. However, the tracks show that the animal was running, often swerving suddenly and sometimes accompanied by a parallel set of prints, and since they are more common in the early part of the year perhaps it is courtship behaviour: the doe being chased, confronted and chased again by a buck. Another sign, which marks the spot where a group of rabbits have been feeding, is the jumbled print where a rabbit thumped its hind feet down as a warning sign.

While rabbits are common on established dunes, snakes are more unusual, but to find the beautiful track made by one sliding down or moving across a dune is the highlight of any outing. It is a rare occurrence for both the adder and the grass snake do not generally frequent such habitats. Although if there are marshy areas within the dune system the latter occasionally is found there.

Whatever the weather, a walk over the dunes is a stimulating experience, made ever more so if you are observing the tracks and signs which abound, while listening to the lark song, sea-birds and the faint melody of waders in a distant estuary.

FIELD-WORK

Observe some footprints and tracks and try to deduce simple behaviour from what you see. Spend a summer day botanizing among the dunes, recognizing a few of the more common flowers and pondering on the unusual ones. Walk through a dune system (many have special walkways to conserve the habitat from human pressure). Obtain permission to visit one of the dune bird colonies of black-headed gulls, terns or herring gulls and watch all the activity, you may well be surprised at the noise, movement, squabbles and sheer beauty of it all. Many places have special hides for

SIGNATURE IN THE SAND

The soft sea sound of a small surf breaking over the beach; fluting oystercatchers alighting among silent gulls; the rustle of marram touched to movement by the gentlest of dawn winds – each an integral part of the dune scene. All around were the signs of the wind's passing; the undulating panorama of sand sculpted into infinite curves and shadowed hollows. Etched into stark outline by the low-angled sun, the tracks of the night creatures had left their signatures in the sand. Fox, rabbit and crow were easy to read, but one was a mystery. It stretched up the slope of a dune as if someone had pressed a long, necklace chain lightly into the sand. Intriguing, baffling, the perpetrator long since departed and now the fingers of the wind were rolling sand grains into the hollows as if intent on keeping the secret. By the time the first sunbeam warmed the dune, all signs of the passer-by had merged into the everchanging scene.

watchers. Sit quietly and listen to the lark song and the cacophony of sea-birds nearby. Spring, summer, autumn and winter each offers its special interest, for dunes always spring surprises.

SITES TO VISIT

Since permits are sometimes required to visit sites, write in the first instance to addresses given below. If you write, please enclose return postage.

Holkham, Norfolk
Regional Officer, NCC, 60 Bracondale, Norwich, Norfolk NR1 2BE.

Saltfleet by Theddlethorpe Dunes
Regional Officer, NCC, Northminster House, Peterborough PE1 1UA.

Lindisfarne, Northumberland
Regional Officer, NCC, Archbold House, Archbold Terrace, Newcastle-upon-Tyne NE2 1EG.

Ainsdale Sand Dunes
Regional Officer, NCC, Blackwell, Bowness-on-Windermere, Windermere, Cumbria LA23 3JR.

Newborough Warren, Ynys Llanddwyn, Anglesey
Regional Officer, NCC, Plas Penrhos, Ffordd Penrhos, Bangor, Gwynedd LL57 2LQ.

Forvie, Grampian Region
Reserve Warden, Wynne-Edwards House, 17 Rubislaw Terrace, Aberdeen AB1 1XE.

Tentsmuir Point, NE Fife
Senior Warden, 46 Crossgate, Cupar, KY15 5HS.

Dungeness, Kent
RSPB Warden, Boulderwall Farm, Dungeness Road, Lydd, Romney Marsh TN29 9PN. Common and sandwich terns with black-headed gulls and a few pairs of the rare Mediterranean gull.

DOWN THE ESTUARY

*You do not know what you may find each day; perhaps you may
only pick up a fallen feather, but it is beautiful, every filament.
Always beautiful! everything beautiful.*

RICHARD JEFFERIES

The best estuaries are wild places where misty distances hold limitless prospects of waders at the tide's edge; places where sand and mud are shaped by river's flood and sea surf; where rolling cloudscapes hold the midday sunlight and where the night sky is a vault of sparkling stars. But they are dangerous places for the unwary, where soft quicksands can trap the careless walker, where the muds have 'boat or barge-wallows', places where the mud is treacherously soft; and where a flood tide can sneak up behind you and cut off your return to the land. But with care, common sense and a little local advice, estuaries are great places to explore.

In winter the estuary will be thronged with sea-birds and waders and the best way to watch is to choose a rising tide as this drives the birds inshore, closer to the estuary edge where you lie in wait. Since many wetland areas are now nature reserves, some of the best have properly constructed hides where you can observe in comparative comfort. (Binoculars are almost indispensable and a good pair of 8×40 or 10×50 are recommended. The first figure indicates the magnification and the second is the size of the front lens in millimetres. Go to a well-established firm or take advice from an experienced birdwatcher as a few minutes' discussion may save you hours of frustration later. And remember, lightness, ease of holding and smooth focussing are important considerations once you have decided how much you can afford.)

What can you expect to see? Most obvious will be the gulls: herring, black-backs, great black-backs and black-headed all come in from the sea in search of food. If there is some sand in the inter-tidal area there will be cockles, sometimes as many as one thousand per square metre, and herring gulls have learned how to cash in on this rich food source. The bird walks over the sand searching for a half-buried cockle which it deftly digs out with a few jabs of its beak. It seizes the shell in its beak and flies up to about 60ft (18m), stalls and releases the shellfish which smashes on to the sand and usually the shell breaks into many pieces. Down comes the gull to feed on the exposed shellfish. You will see evidence of this feeding practice in the broken shells scattered around and the large gull footprints nearby, but with a little perseverance you can watch it all happen. Carrion crows seem to have discovered this method of food gathering and a solitary crow will be seen repeating the action quite successfully. Did the crow copy the actions of the gull, or was the practice discovered by accident? A point to ponder.

Oystercatchers, or sea-pies, also thrive on cockles and where these shellfish are abundant an oystercatcher will consume as many as five hundred cockles in a single day, or the equivalent of nearly half its body weight. In a single year an oystercatcher may eat up to one hundred and fifty times its own weight in cockles! So as you watch the bird digging out those cockles try to appreciate the total bulk moved in a year: if we include the weight of

Watch and listen to oystercatchers as they feed.

Out on the banks at low tide, cormorants rest after hunting fish out in the tideways, looking almost heraldic with black wings outstretched in the wind to dry their plumage. One of the problems facing a novice birdwatcher is how to differentiate between a cormorant and a shag. Generally speaking the cormorant has a white chin whereas the shag has no visible white markings; in the breeding season the latter has a curved crest of feathers on its head. While cormorants frequent sea and estuary, the shag tends to favour the seas around rocky coasts and is only a rare visitor to most estuaries. Nevertheless, a highly experienced birdwatcher once professed that he was not sure whether 'that shagorant might not be a cormorag'. Feeding cormorants are worth watching and it is quite a good exercise in observation to distinguish the species of fish caught: you have about four to six seconds when it surfaces, before the head is tossed and the fish swallowed. It will probably be difficult

the shell then a single oystercatcher carries and breaks open nearly a tonne and a half of shells and their contents. A staggering amount for a bird weighing less than $1\frac{1}{2}$lb (3kg).

Signs of oystercatcher feeding are the large piles of broken cockle shells formed when the bird removes cockles from the sand and carries them to a patch of hard sand where they are hammered open by its powerful beak. This practice is easily observed on most sandy areas of estuaries.

Fortunately for the cockle's survival, it spawns when a year old and can live to ten years of age, spawning enormous numbers of fry each year. So there are always plenty of cockles despite the attentions of herring gulls, oystercatchers and human beings – all gathering a tasty meal. If you examine the shell of a cockle you will see a number of growth rings and from these you can tell its age; although sometimes a ring forms when the cockle suffers some form of disturbance, but generally these rings are a fairly close guide to its age.

Because they become waterlogged when deep diving, cormorants need to dry out periodically.

to tell whether the flatfish is a plaice or a flounder, but scorpion fish are easy to recognize, if only because it takes the bird a little longer to swallow the spiked head.

Winter is, without doubt, *the* best time for estuary watching, for then wildfowl flight in to join a growing number of waders moving in from their breeding areas. Knot, dunlin, curlew and bar-tailed godwit feed in the pools at low tide and you will probably also find shelduck sieving through the mud. If there is eel grass or enteromorpha growing in the vicinity you will see brent geese – unmistakable small, dark-bellied, black-plumaged birds with neat white collars. They spend much of the day browsing on these plants and it is worth spending an hour watching these handsome birds that have made the long journey from Arctic Siberia.

Other geese such as the pinkfeet geese seek out low-tide sand or mud banks as safe night roosting places. Among the smaller birds, the ringed plover with its prominent black collar and black and white head pattern runs about in short bursts, pausing to pick up small invertebrates.

Since there are more waders in the estuary in the non-breeding season, it is obviously better to go there in the winter. They feed between high- and low-tide marks and their diet consists largely of shellfish, crustaceans and marine worms; these exist in vast numbers in the birds' favoured feeding grounds. The populations of certain ragworms eaten by small waders may be as dense as six hundred to a square metre; a small crustacean (*Corophium volutator*), as many as twenty thousand and a tiny shellfish (*Hydrobia ulvae*), the astronomical number of over forty thousand. Look for hydrobia, which is a tiny 5mm snail-like shellfish, as the tide ebbs off the mud. Search on the edge of the water and you will see them speckling the surface; but quite soon, as the mud begins to dry, they all bury and disappear. When the tide returns they come up to the surface and launch out on the surface film aided by a mucous mat which also gathers plankton on which they feed. They drift inshore and then as the tide again ebbs the entire cycle begins over again. Thus

ESTUARY DAWN

Dawn came slowly out of the grey sea, tracing hints of light over the ice-coated runnels as the first glimmers were captured in the rimed heads of the rushes and the mud, whence the ebb tide had retreated. Out on the mussel beds a few oystercatchers stirred, their flute-like pipings sharp and clear on the frosty air.

A curlew winged past, its echoing voice growing fainter, calling to others over the tide's edge, where the gulls rose into the growing light on lazy wings to blend with the winter dawn and head inland for the plough.

Soft sounds of distant surf mellowed the whistling of a cock wigeon; a redshank, that sentinel of the estuary and marsh, cried its warning where a crabbing boat passed *en route* for distant waters. In the half light, black specks on the distant sand bar lifted into formation and borne on the wind, came the soul-stirring clamour of geese. Majestically the skein winged in to set the reeds vibrating with the threshing beat of their great wings and the morning thrilled to the crescendo of wild goose call – music that held the magic of the northlands. Those great grey birds, crying wildly in the winter dawn, had skeined over lands beyond our knowing. Their elemental calls echoing wilderness beyond imagination and as they vanished towards the distant stubble fields their haunting refrain faded into the sighing of wind and the murmur of the flood tide rising to another day.

their tidal movements are followed by the feeding waders.

In time, as the estuary becomes more familiar and the best times of season, day, night and tide are understood, some of the rarer moments will be enjoyed. Moments to savour such as watching an Arctic skua trailing its long, straight feathers from a wedge-shaped tail, chasing a gull that has some unswallowed food in its beak. The skua follows every twist and turn of the gull, worrying it until the gull drops the food, or in many cases actually causes the gull to disgorge its previous meal. Another exciting sight is that of the short-eared owl hunting with silent, slow wing beats and occasional glides along the edge of the estuary. It is a bird that hunts by day as well as the dusk-time favoured by other owls. Then, as winter loosens its grip, the first tentative courtship displays and behaviour will begin. These are often moments of high drama and certainly beauty, as the birds prepare for the nesting season and their eventual departure from the estuary.

Sorting out the names of the waders is not an easy job for so many of them look like 'little brown birds'; the best advice is to take your time. Instead of trying to cope with ten different kinds, choose one and concentrate on that one alone. Then, using one of the field guides listed in the reference section, begin by comparing what you are observing with pictures and then descriptions until you get tolerably close to a positive identification. Now start looking for colour of legs and beak or particular plumage markings, its flight pattern and voice when calling. By spending an hour or so watching one species of bird and referring to descriptions you will find future recognition of that bird a simple matter. The great moment of achievement will come quite suddenly one day when you hear a bird call in the distance or see one fly over a mussel bank and you *recognize* it. Instant recognition is perhaps one of the great rewards of observ-

ation – familiarity with the 'jizz' of a bird is just reward for patient hours watching its movements, feeding pattern, seasonal presence in a certain habitat, plumage changes, sexual differences and all the salient factors that make a redshank a redshank and a greenshank a greenshank.

While it is not my intention to talk about rarities there is one bird that really does deserve a mention. That lovely, graceful bird is the avocet which was extinct as a breeding species in this country for nearly one hundred years. Then a small colony became established on Havergate Island and later the RSPB had extraordinary success with a colony in their reserve at Minsmere. Between July and October or April to June you may be fortunate enough to see some migrants in Suffolk, Norfolk, Kent, Sussex and Hampshire. A few birds overwinter on the estuaries of Devon and Cornwall where special 'Avocet Cruises' are organized. Today, when the list of disappearing species grows longer year by year, it is exciting to know that a once-extinct breeding species is successfully increasing in parts of our country.

As you become familiar with a particular estuary you will almost certainly find the waders' roost. Each day as the tide rises the

KEY TO PAGES 54–55
A few of those 'brown birds' among the estuary waders:
1 black-tailed godwit; 2 bar-tailed godwit; 3 redshank;
4 ringed plover; 5 curlew; 6 knots.

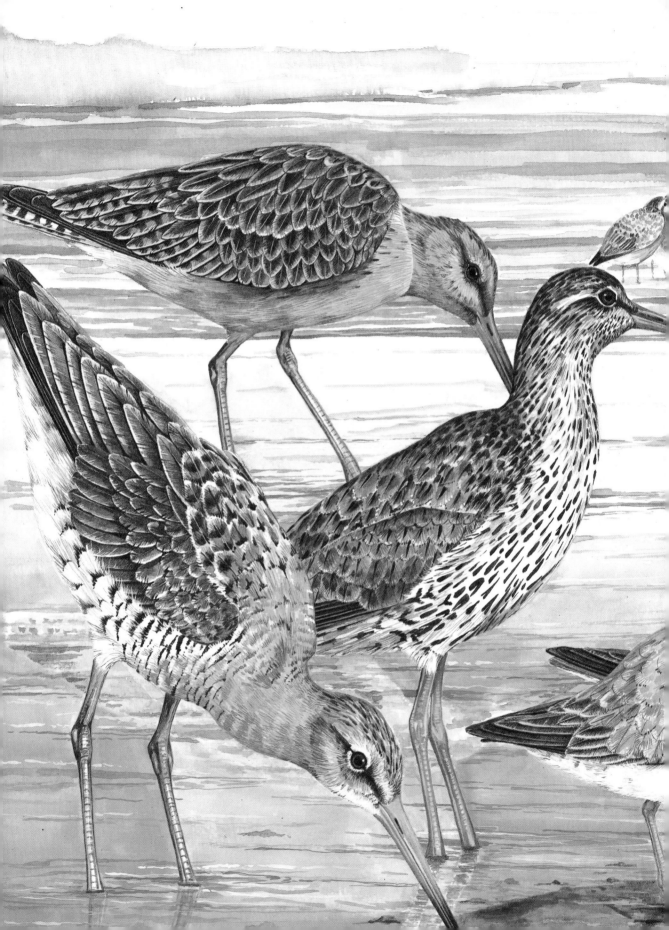

birds move in with the flood tide, but eventually the rising waters cover the mudflats and all but the highest raised banks. It is to these that the waders finally retreat, to rest, preen and then sleep, safe from most predators. It is a wonderful sight to see a roost with perhaps thousands of birds clustered together so closely that some of the smaller ones are almost between the legs of the larger. Just before they finally settle down, whole flocks take to the air, wheeling, turning, climbing and then alighting – a marvellous sight seen against a setting sun, with ever-changing patterns etched against the sky. It is this part of the spirit of the estuary that enters the blood and you find yourself returning again and again to be with the birds, to witness a scene that endures despite the passing of time.

FIELD-WORK

For occasional weekends, visit a number of local estuaries. You will find the variation quite stimulating if only because there is that air of expectancy in not knowing what you might see. If you favour a particular site, go there in different seasons so as to appreciate the remarkable differences between winter and summer, spring and autumn. Why not follow some of your favourite birds to their summer breeding grounds – not perhaps to the Siberian Arctic, but to local moorland or marsh.

Look for shells opened by oystercatchers, gulls and waders and take a close look at the tiny hydrobia that helps sustain all those birds. Visit the estuary edge after dark; listen to the calls, whistle of pinions and all the other intriguing sounds – try recording some of them. Go down to the estuary before dawn, watch the first light and enjoy the flight of wildfowl and waders going about their daily life. And in your armchair read some of those wonderfully evocative books by Peter Scott, 'BB' (with D J Watkins-Pitchford's atmospheric drawings), Ian Niall, and *Hunters Fen* by John Humphreys. Such atmospheric writing is almost guaranteed to turn every browser into an avid observer.

SITES TO VISIT

Our coastline is studded with so many beautiful estuaries that there is certain to be one within easy reach by car.

The RSPB book *Reserves Visiting* gives very detailed information on their reserves, many of which are particularly attractive because of the variety of species and the presence of suitable hides. The book is obtainable from Reserves Division, Royal Society for the Protection of Birds, The Lodge, Sandy, Bedfordshire SG19 2DL (Tel: 0767 80551).

Nigg & Udale Bays, Ross & Cromarty
Five thousand acres of intertidal flats of international importance for migratory wildfowl. Varieties and numbers of all types of birds present are paralleled in few other estuarine sites in the UK.

Dyfi, Dyfed (Ceredigion)
Regional Officer, NCC Plas Gogerddan, Aberystwyth, Dyfed SY23 3EB. River estuary, dune system and raised bog. Contact above before visiting.

THROUGH THE REEDS

Light and freedom, colour and delicious air – sunshine, blue hill
lines and flowers – give the heart to feel that there is so much more
to be enjoyed of which we walk in ignorance.

RICHARD JEFFERIES

The fascination of any stretch of water lies in its potential to surprise the observer; to offer unusual sights and happenings that can occur suddenly and quite unexpectedly; to delight with its infinite variety and the constantly changing interplay between sunlight-created water reflections quenched in wind-flurries, and the colourful behaviour of the water-loving birds that live there.

Brilliantly beautiful both in plumage and behaviour, the great crested grebe in the breeding season is a delight to behold. Their courtship displays rank among the most spectacular in the bird world, and one of the best sites to see them is often the man-created gravel pits, many of which have now been converted into nature reserves. When you find a pair of grebes, stay awhile and watch as they run over the water together or dive simultaneously. Then collecting pieces of water weed, they swim together to offer the plants, each to the other, as a bonding of their partnership which eventually leads to nest building.

As with all wildlife watching, one of the secrets is to melt into the surroundings, keeping very still and quiet and then simply wait for things to happen. When you first walk into the scene you can be quite sure that every bird on the water or on the shores has seen you. The natural reaction of those birds on the shore and those seeking cover in the reeds is to remain in hiding as long as you remain mobile; those on the lake will be watching you, for alas, humans are always regarded as a threat, and they will continue to watch you as long as

your behaviour is fidgety. Perhaps one of the most important guides to wildlife watching is to realize that animals possess an extremely acute perception of danger or threat. Their eyes and hearing are finely tuned to the normal, everyday sights and sounds of their habitat and the smallest intrusion of alien presence is detected immediately. The observer must always be aware of toleration distance – the distance between the animal and observer which each species accepts as 'safe' – respect that distance and you will be tolerated, encroach further and the animal will retreat. You can test this theory by watching quite common birds standing on ground ahead of your walking line. A blackbird's 'toleration distance' is close to 20ft (6m), whereas a magpie will take flight if an intruder gets within 150ft (45m) of its position. So, bearing all this in mind, find a comfortable place to sit, perhaps partially screened by bushes or tall grass, or watch through the reeds.

Richard Jefferies, a man always in tune with nature, knew that most wildlife reacts favourably towards us providing we respect it. He wrote:

> From the tiniest insect upwards they are so ready to dwell in sympathy with us – only be tender, quiet, considerate, in a word, gentlemanly, towards them and they will freely wander around. And they have all such marvellous tales to tell – intricate problems to solve for us.

Whether you choose to sit in contemplation,

Great crested grebes courting.

or in observation, there is always much to see, especially during February and March when the mallard will be busy displaying. Have you ever stopped to really look at the plumage of the male mallard on a sunny morning? The shimmering, iridescent green of its head and the shining bright-yellow bill separated from its rusty-red breast by a clean, white collar are certainly worth close inspection, and the grey of its body is speckled beauty far removed from our normal concept of grey. Because the mallard is so common, and usually associated with 'duck ponds', we tend to overlook its beauty and fail to realize that large numbers of them are truly wild. They can all be recognized by their rather large size and the bright-blue speculum bordered by white and black. This speculum is a patch of coloured feathers on the wing which, when the bird is not flying, shows up on the side of the body towards the tail end.

A wide variety of ducks will frequent the lake through most of the year so take a good field guide with you and start sorting out the surface-feeders and diving ducks. While watching the latter you could time the duration underwater for a number of dives and also the length of interval between dives. Recording facts like this will add interest to your duck watching and enable you to have a

Mallard feeding.

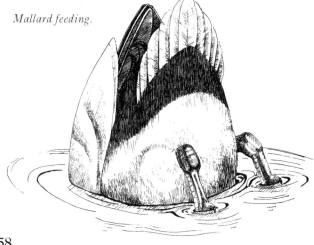

Diving ducks: tufted (left) and pochard.

greater understanding of the bird's private life. I suggest you begin by observing the tufted duck. Try to keep a diary of observed happenings. Most naturalists keep a diary which can be as detailed or sketchy as you choose, but many newcomers to the gentle art of observation fail to grasp the fact that much of what they see may never have been recorded before. So much is unknown, so limited our knowledge of even the commonest species, that every observed act of behaviour may one day help to complete the jig-saw puzzle of a particular creature's life.

As an addition to your watching activities you may find it useful to become involved with a co-operative survey or census. From time to time organizations like the British Trust for Ornithology, Royal Society for the Protection of Birds or the Wildfowl Trust carry out national counts on a certain day, or over a given period, and they need the assistance of a large number of volunteers. For instance, there may be a census of ducks on inland waters, and from the correlated results of the observations a picture of the status of ducks in such habitats is recorded. Repeating the census over a period of years will indicate rises or falls in populations within those habitats. This of course is only an example

and in reality a whole range of interesting and co-operative work is undertaken in this way. By getting in touch with the relevant organization you will hear all about what is going on and be able to join in. Such scientific work, although basic, adds immense interest to your observations and you will meet fellow watchers whose experiences provide hours of conversation and make possible the exchange of information.

Two water birds well worth watching are the coot and moorhen, but both are extremely shy and wary. The coot is generally much the commoner bird and can be recognized by its black plumage and white shield sweeping up from its white bill. Although it is not a good flier and takes off with a great and noisy pattering of its feet along the surface, it quite frequently goes out into the middle of a lake. If disturbed when some distance from the nearest reeds, it usually runs fast on the water, pushing with its feet and using its wings to keep it just above the water. The clatter it makes can be heard from a great distance. It feeds on underwater plants which it collects by giving a little jump and then diving beneath the surface, often staying down for as long as half a minute. It is particularly interesting to watch when it is on the water with young; each parent will dive and then surface with water-weed which they drop on the water surface and watch as the young feed.

The moorhen has brownish-black plumage with white stripes on its side. Its beak is red at its base with a red frontal shield. Unlike the coot it feeds on the land, often some distance from the water. If it sees you it will run for the water where it will swim up and down close to cover. It sometimes climbs into bushes, not solely to roost but in season to feed on the berries or seeds. Like the coot it finds flight difficult, taking off by running along the surface for some considerable distance before becoming airborne.

You may find some reed warblers living among the reeds, they are summer visitors who build their nests suspended between reeds. It is a lovely structure which started life as a few strands of dry, dead reed leaf woven around the stems of a few reeds. Strands of long moss are then placed to form a platform, and into this and around the stems further lengths of leaf are threaded. It is a tricky business and a delicate structure, and often the nests are damaged when gales of wind set the reed canes swaying. When sheep are pastured nearby, their wool is often incorpo-

rated with occasional long stems of grasses. Reed warblers are often the victims of cuckoos and then the small warblers have an unexpectedly busy time feeding their large parasite. Their work load is particularly heavy because the birds gather small midges, flies and aphids and it must take many of these to satisfy the hunger of a growing cuckoo. But they also catch dragonflies, damselflies, the long-legged crane fly and even worms, so no doubt these help to satisfy their gorging intruder.

If the lake is near the sea, herring gulls, black-headed gulls and cormorants flight in. The latter often perch on a tree or post where they stretch their wings out to dry, while the gulls bathe quite vigorously in the fresh water. Have you ever observed gulls alighting on fresh water? The first thing they do is dip their beak in to taste it – it is too brief an action for the birds to be drinking. Later when they fly off they shake their body and tail to rid it of moisture. You may feel such simple observations are worthless, yet they are important

Stay awhile to watch the cygnets feeding.

*While the great crested newt is a threatened species, the smooth
newt and palmate newt are fairly common.*

pieces of the jigsaw and well worth recording, for life is a very intricate process. There is, of course, always a tendency to become 'blinkered', to be so obsessed with the behaviour of a particular bird, mammal, insect or reptile that we fail to see what is happening nearby, or even at a distance – a happening that may be modifying or triggering the behaviour on which we are concentrating. I remember walking the shore with a friend, an electrician, who once complained, as we came up to the promenade, that I always saw the living creatures, whereas all he saw were pieces of electric wire and broken electric light bulbs.

As I write I can hear a herring gull uttering its warning call on a roof a hundred metres away; while a few minutes ago a starling was giving a perfect imitation of a curlew from the roof opposite; a greenfly has just alighted on a nearby leaf; and a spider is busy wrapping a captured fly in silk in its web on the window; two blackbirds are defending their territories on the lawn and honeybees are busy in the hybrid heathers in the border. All this is happening to the background of traffic and a distant transistor, yet with practice it is not difficult to exclude the unwanted ephemera and tune in to the interesting subject matter.

Back on the lake, on a still day, with a pair of polaroid glasses and from a good vantage point, a whole range of underwater activities can be observed. Perhaps a shoal of fish fry will swim by in the shallows; among the pondweed larvae will be feeding and adult water beetles will come to the surface for air. Dragonflies will alight and there will be stoneflies and caddisflies to be observed. Turn over a stone in the shallow margin and perhaps a leech will move off as only a leech can and, despite its rather unpleasant reputation it is, nevertheless, a beautiful creature wonderfully adapted to its way of life. You may even be fortunate to see thirty or forty baby leeches hitching a ride on the adult. And see too, on that same stone, the delicately built home of a caddis larva. Each tiny grain of sand, snail shell or stem fragment accurately secured in a precise position with a silk-like secretion which also forms a smooth lining to its tube.

Flowers, according to season, adorn the lake surface Springtime sees the brilliant

The difference: moorhen (left) and coot.

yellow cups of the kingcups or marsh marigold, pink spikes of amphibious bistort, white water-lily and the pretty yellow water-lily, tiny blue forget-me-nots, in summer; while midsummer finds the tall purple loosestrife with its bright red-purple flowers growing from shallow water on to the edge of the shoreline. There are so many flowers that it would be tedious to list them all. Flowers, like other wildlife, need to be enjoyed in their natural habitat where one can slowly become acquainted with them and their flowering times; once recognized you can seek them out each succeeding year bringing their fragile beauty to enhance the water scene.

This seasonal awareness can become one of the most satisfying aspects of nature study for, wherever you go, you will find yourself looking for the familiar happening: the first celandine; stitchwort sparkling in the hedge; rooks carrying nest material; woodpeckers drumming; the first fledgling on the lawn; autumn colours; the first frost or frog and toad spawn in the marshy pool. Each in its own way contributes to a living calendar of the ever-changing seasons, and to the pleasure you will experience as an observer of the natural world.

FIELD-WORK

Visit a nearby stretch of fresh water, for example a lake or reservoir, and compare the two seasons. Write off to one of the wildlife organizations mentioned in the text and if they are planning a census, you could join them.

Take a pair of polaroid glasses so that you may see more distinctly through the water. If you have a tape recorder, try recording some of the sounds and make a sound record of your visit.

Photograph some of the waterside flowers. Why not start a nature diary? Record what you see in words and small sketches. Try to visit a lake or reservoir in the duck-breeding season and watch their patterns of courtship behaviour.

Turn over a few stones near the bank and

look for caddis larvae and leeches. Remember to return the stone to its original position so as not to disturb small creatures that have made their home there.

HALF A MILLION STARLINGS

In the fading light we eased the dinghy through the tall phragmites, their strong, bamboo-like stems reluctantly parting as the bows penetrated deeper. We anchored, set up our prepared camouflage cover and relaxed to wait. Half an hour passed and then quite suddenly the blood-red sky became mottled with thousands of tiny black dots, merging nearby into flowing lines, sweeping masses and rhythmic movements. The starlings were coming; coming to their roost in the reed bed where we waited.

Before the first owl called in the wood across the lake, the great flock winged in overhead, the downdraught of their wings setting the reeds in motion. They alighted, all around us, conversing and chattering, keeping in contact, before rushing upwards once more to wheel and scream above the reeds. Several times this happened until, finally, they stayed down and half a million birds set the evening air pulsating with the beating of half a million tiny hearts – the breathing of myriad starlings. So much delicate life settling down to sleep, as if we were enveloped by a mantle of feathers; our very being suffused with their quietening animation. Then, slowly, peace wandered through the reeds, touching their eyelids with sleep, safe from predators and unaware of our presence.

Reed warbler with a three-week-old cuckoo, now weighing ten times its hatching weight.

ALONG THE RIVERBANK

Never omit to explore a footpath, for never was there a footpath yet
which did not pass something of interest.
RICHARD JEFFERIES

An afternoon's walk beside a river can be full of surprises for anyone on the watch for wildlife, but like observing life in any habitat the secret lies in unobtrusiveness and in being prepared to spend a little time being quiet and still. River-watching can soon become a habit, especially if we choose to explore the upper reaches of some of our rivers. Generally, the kind of wildlife living in and near a river will depend on whether the river is fast flowing through upland areas or slow flowing through lowland flood plains. Speed of flow profoundly affects the plant growth, the nature of the river bed and banks and all the micro-habitats that develop in consequence. Such differences become very obvious if we compare the moorland reach running between bracken-covered banks with, a little later, the same stream rolling under woodland trees and ferns along the banks, and then a lowland reach where the river is wide and either flowing through water meadows where plants and flowers abound or sliding through dense reed-beds, as on the Norfolk Broads.

One of the most amazing sights in fast-running water is a dipper hunting for food. It is a small bird, only about 7in (18cm) long, and throughout the year may be found either singly or in pairs occupying the same piece of territory. They favour river stretches where the water tumbles through gaps between large boulders and where long glides of rippled water flow over a sandy bottom, interspersed with small pools formed by fallen trees or where tumbled rocks form an improvized dam. More often than not, you will come upon the bird by chance as it flies low over the surface and alights on a moss-covered boulder, in mid-stream. Here it bobs and 'curtsys', seesawing its body with tail flicking downwards in a quite unmistakable manner. If it is going to feed it will soon walk quickly down the rock to the edge of the water, float for a fraction of a second and then dive. Now comes the most surprising behaviour of all: *it walks along the river bed*. If you keep still, perhaps behind the cover of alder buckthorn, gorse or even bracken, with a little luck, where the water runs clear, you can see this quite plainly. Down below it picks up all kinds of aquatic insects and their larvae, small fish and other small denizens of the river. With its white breast edged below with dark chestnut and a black back with tail stuck up like a wren it looks a tough little bird, thriving in what may seem rather extreme conditions.

Another way of finding these little birds is in the breeding season, between late February and April. Choose a small stone bridge or a likely place and sit and watch. You may well see one nest-building or, if it is later in the season, feeding its young. Like all bird-watching it requires experience to know where to find a dipper, but surely half the fun is going out and searching. Not every trip will be successful, but you will see much of interest on the way, and one day, bobbing on a rock by the running water, you *will* see a dipper, and that will be a moment to remember.

The brightest star of the river is the kingfisher, which in flight zips past, a pale blue streak against the glittering water. It will take time to discover its haunts, although it is quite common on some rivers. Where small fish are bountiful a kingfisher will often perch on a bough over the water, leap off, hover for a brief moment, head and beak pointing towards the water before plunging in. Fish in beak it flies back to its perch, tosses the fish round and swallows it head first. Once again anglers will tell you where to look, although many of them regard the bird as a pest. However, our countryside would be a duller place without their tropical colours gracing our streams.

Another bird that tends to be found among the river's upper reaches is the grey wagtail, with its blue-grey back and upper parts and yellow breast and under tail. It is another tail-bobber but this one is distinctive because the tail is so long, and the bird is often seen flitting along the side of streams to alight on a sandy bank or rock, and that is when the tail goes into motion, constantly bobbing.

But surely the most elegant and elusive river bird is the heron, tall and majestic with a long slim neck and legs like dried reed stems. It stands motionless in the shade of a willow or among reeds, and the first view is often of the bird flapping away on huge wings, head between shoulders and legs trailing behind, disappearing from sight to alight again some two hundred metres further on. It is extremely difficult to get close to a heron, but the best time is dawn or late evening, which seems to be a favoured fishing time. If you can watch from a car so much the better, but if you have to approach on foot keep in cover and then observe through binoculars because in open ground it flies off as soon as you get within 250ft (75m). Like all birds it has its own 'toleration distance', that is the closest it will permit you to approach, and like many living animals and birds, it is always possible to get a little closer if you look a little to one side of it. Never stare or make eye contact in a direct confrontation, no matter how far away

you happen to be. By making enquiries from water-bailiffs, river boards or anglers you should be able to locate a heronry. From early February to March you can see the birds nest building and performing some of their ritual displays high in the tree-tops, and later in the year see (and hear!) them feeding their young.

As an observer of behaviour you will want to cover as many aspects of the heron's life as possible. Where does it go to feed, and what does it eat; how does it react and interact with other members of the heronry; how does it display and maintain the pair-bond; what are its methods of feeding the young; what nesting materials does it use; when and how does it preen? If you only answer a few of these questions, you will begin to acquire a deeper knowledge of the bird's way of life, and that can be deeply satisfying.

If the heron is the largest river bird, one of the smaller ones is the little grebe or dabchick. It spends much of its time diving for small fish, shellfish and water insects, staying down for twelve or more seconds. They are shy little birds and if frightened will surface with only the head above water or seek cover among stream-side vegetation.

Most river watchers like to look for fish, and looking for fish in fast-running water is a pastime that becomes more rewarding as the habits of the fish become better known. That may sound obvious, and indeed it is, so take a fast upland river as an example, and for the fish we will study a trout. By looking carefully at the water you will soon notice that a number of large boulders protrude through the surface. Such rocks cause the running water to part into two swift currents so that behind the rock is a V-shaped area of comparatively still water. It is here that the trout often lie in wait for food being borne past in the current. From the point of view of the fish, it is obviously advantageous to rest in quiet water as it does not involve the continuous expenditure of energy that would be necessary in fast-running water. So, firstly, look in just such a place and if you have a pair of polaroid glasses observation becomes easier – it is quite astonishing what can be seen through water by wearing these glasses, the entire habitat leaps into focus with a three-dimensional quality. Secondly, look for the shadow-shape of the fish – trout have a beautifully camouflaged body which renders them virtually invisible when viewed from above. So look for the shadow (undulating shadows usually denote a fish) and high places such as bridges make good vantage points for observation.

During the winter months it is possible to witness a marvellous spectacle on our salmon rivers as the salmon come in from the sea and swim up-river. From mid October to the end of November, salmon can be seen jumping in stretches of fast-running water with plenty of rocks and obstructions such as weirs and dams. The best conditions to observe this incredible test of strength and determination are after heavy rain when the river is in full spate, running fast and high. For information on the best places to see the 'salmon leap' consult local anglers or a fishing-tackle shop in the vicinity of a good salmon river.

ABOVE:
A rainbow-flash over the clear stream – the kingfisher.

OPPOSITE:
The 'walker on the river bed', the dipper, flies up to feed its nestlings.

A pulsating shadow, the first sign of a trout.

In quieter waters there is a little animal that lives in the banks of slow-running streams and rivers that is an ideal subject for a spell of mammal watching – the water vole. They vary in size and colour in different parts of the country, in Scotland, for instance, they are smaller and darker than those found further south, but all are delightful little creatures. Animals are always suspicious of humans and extremely sensitive to any form of intrusion or disturbance, but water voles, having been left well alone by us and not persecuted in any way, do not regard us as an enemy. Having found a likely stream, to observe water voles search the banks for their burrow entrances. Move your feet lightly and

Quiet and patient observation rewarded as a water vole emerges.

remember that vibrations from your move-ments will be transmitted through the soil and water. Ideally you will be wearing a coat that is warm and quiet – unfortunately many plasticized anoraks and waterproofs make 'scratchy' noises whenever you move and alert wildlife to your presence. Hide if you wish, but these little animals will carry on with their business as long as you keep still and quiet. Before you sit down, peel a fresh apple and throw a few small pieces near their burrow entrance on the opposite bank and soon a vole will appear.

Water voles feed both on the bank and from the stream, but they never feed far from the water. Your first sight may be of the little animal having a scratch and general look around to make sure all is safe. Then it sets about eating by biting through a stem, hold-ing it in the forepaws and munching away at the grass which is its staple diet. If it is quiet and you listen carefully you will hear the 'plop' as a water vole dives into the water and with just a little luck you might be able to watch it swimming. Sitting by a stream in the water-scented summer air watching these fascinating little creatures is worth all the time spent in discovery.

FIELD-WORK

Walk along the bank of a river and, if it is fast flowing, watch for a dipper. Take a pair of polaroid glasses and while you are searching, look closely into the water for fish. If it is a slow-flowing stream try to discover some water-vole burrows and spend an hour watch-ing them. Locate your nearest heronry and visit it during the breeding season in March, or test your skill in stalking by approaching and then observing a feeding heron. Look for the many riverside birds and identify them from a good field guide. In summer watch the drag-onflies in flight, feeding, maintaining terri-tory, mating and egg-laying.

EARTH-BORN STARS

It had been one of those evenings which was specifically created for a walk beside the river. Such was the beauty of the scene we felt compelled to stay awhile and watch as dusk quenched the sparkling water. The coming of darkness holds its own magic, which is released slowly to those who enjoy the wildlife night-scene. Soon the moonless sky was velvet over the tree-tops as we waited for the badgers, but in their own inimitable way they were late. Half an hour passed and then suddenly in the grass on the river bank flashed a yellow-green spark. In a moment or two it flashed again, and then again, and slowly as my eyes grew accustomed a score of sparks twinkled by the river. Glow-worms. Females all, burn-ing their courtship lights to attract males. Yet what extraordinary light it is, a small miracle of production having a transparent outer layer which produces the illumin-ation by a chemical reaction and an inner reflecting layer that ensures maximum in-tensity. But the amazing wonder of its light is that it is cold and produced by a few chemicals, plus oxygen and water.

Wordsworth called it 'An earth-born star' and beside the river as we watched, his poetry lived again and we sought no under-standing of the light's source, but only watched, with a sense of wonder at its beauty.

SITES TO VISIT

With so many rivers and streams around the countryside, the choice is yours, but some are private fishing waters. It is *always* good policy to obtain permission prior to walking the banks. Most of our rivers are open to the public.

BESIDE THE POND

The true harvest of my daily life is somewhat as intangible and indescribable as the tints of morning or evening. It is a little stardust caught, a segment of the rainbow which I have clutched.

HENRY DAVID THOREAU

Ponds both natural and man-made will provide endless hours for watching water life. But perhaps 'natural' and 'man-made' are ambiguous terms, for the great majority of what may appear to be natural were probably excavated or treated by man centuries ago; by man-made I include the wide variety of plastic and fibre-glass ponds and those made from brick and cement or any other artificial means. What can be found in a pond varies according to where it is situated, its closeness or distance from other water sources, its size, depth and general characteristics such as vegetation, soil and age. The latter being of great importance for there is a vast difference between the extent of life in a new pond and in one with well-established vegetation. Because its limits are so confined, a pond is a world in miniature in which the entire gamut of plants and animals are interdependent. The animals range in size from microscopic single-celled creatures called protozoa to the quite sizeable fish that are at the top of the food chain.

One cardinal rule to be observed when pond-watching is to approach slowly and as quietly as possible, avoid any vibrations that may warn the creatures and send them heading for cover. Fish of all kinds are very sensitive to movement, so avoid casting a shadow over the water and once you are at the pond-side make yourself comfortable and settle down to watch.

KEY TO PAGES 70–71
If you sit still, the dragonflies will come very close and you will be able to observe their behaviour. You might see the following: 1 banded demoiselle damselfly; 2 blue-tailed damselfly; 3 four-spotted chaser; 4 golden-ringed dragonfly; 5 common hawker; 6 common darter; 7 azure damselfly.

During the summer months one of the first insects you are likely to see will be a dragonfly, the horse-stinger or devil's darning needle as they used to be called by country folk years ago. Needless to say, dragonflies cannot sting, simply because they possess no stinging apparatus. Admittedly, if one is held gently between the fingers it will curve its body towards a finger in a way that suggests a stinging attempt, but that is an illusion so this delightful flier can be observed with impunity. And what wonderful fliers they are as they hawk over the water and through the reeds hunting the innumerable flying insects that share the habitat with them. Jefferies knew the dragonflies well:

On the wings of the dragonfly as he hovers an instant before he darts there is a prismatic gleam. These wing textures are even more delicate than the minute filaments on a swallow's quill, more delicate than the pollen of a flower.

I remember watching a large golden-ringed dragonfly as it flew over some tall gorse bushes and in the silence the rustle of its wings could be plainly heard. Suddenly it veered to one side and I actually saw it seize a small bumble (humble if you prefer) bee whose wings set up quite a buzz as it tried to escape. The dragonfly almost immediately alighted on some gorse blooms at the edge of the bush, so I eased around very slowly – for the eyesight of dragonflies is extremely acute – until I was within a metre of it. The bee was almost the size of the dragonfly's head and thorax combined and was securely pinioned in the network of the six spiked legs. Within a minute or so its struggles suddenly ceased as the dragonfly bit through the bee's body, severing the head. At that very moment it saw me and its large head with those shining, beautiful compound eyes swivelled slowly around and then it soared away over the gorse and out of my sight.

Once you become a dragonfly watcher it is not long before you discover that these insects are 'people watchers', for if you approach some species resting, for instance on a tall reed or plant stem, you will observe how they slowly move around the stem and then freeze into immobility as they watch you. Sitting beside the pond on a warm, sunlit, still afternoon you may be fortunate enough to watch a pair egg-laying. The emerald damselfly flies in tandem before mating, the male holding on to the female's neck with his claspers, which are situated at his tail end. The process of fertilization is unique in the insect world. In the male the opening for the sperm is near the tail end but the copulatory apparatus is up near its thorax so prior to mating the male has to transfer his sperm into this section of his body. Having done this he then courts a female by much wing fluttering and hovering near her, before he seizes her neck with his claspers at the tail end of his body. Very soon the female bends her tail upwards to the section where the male has already placed his sperm and so she becomes fertilized. Still in tandem they fly to a reed or similar plant and the female submerges below the surface, often with the male still holding her. She then cuts into the stem in several places, depositing her eggs in the holes so made. Some of the larger dagonflies fly over the water, touching the surface with their 'tail end', so releasing the eggs.

As you become better acquainted with dragonflies you will begin to notice that some species show a territorial instinct. The banded demoiselle male often chooses a prominent twig or leaf and here he will sit and survey the happenings around him, particularly the arrival of insects suitable to eat. Then from his perch he flies, captures his prey and returns to his perch to feed. His territory usually includes a nearby patch of aquatic plants, with some leaves on the surface, because one day he will encounter a female and, in tandem, this is where she will lay her eggs. If another male flies into this territory he will chase it away. It is an absorbing spectacle. These elegant, beautiful and intriguing insects are quite short lived, most species surviving for little more than a few weeks.

Most ponds contain caddisfly larvae and these little creatures live in tubes that they have constructed and lined with silk to which they attach a wide variety of small objects, some using the shell of small snails, others tiny fragments of saturated wood, while others prefer fragments of chewed-off plant stem. Inside these shelters, with only their legs and head protruding, they walk around and climb among the submerged plants. At the first sign of danger they withdrew into the tube.

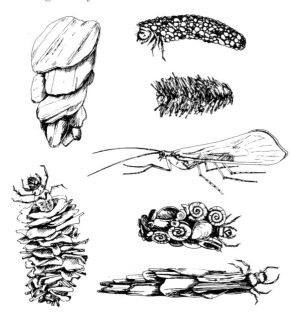

Use a hand lens to see the varied natural objects that caddis larvae use for their homes.

When the surface is calm and still you can watch the whirligig beetles rushing about on the surface film like miniature dodgem cars, apparently crazy for there seems no purpose in their gyrations. In fact, these movements help them to find food and when disturbed by a predator or threat from the bank one will move wildly away causing the others to realize the danger and so dive or scatter to safety. These little creatures are beautifully adapted to life on the pond's surface, for their eyes are divided into two parts, one for viewing life above water and the other for seeing underwater. They are most rewarding to watch and providing you keep still you will be treated to an insect ballet of most unusual liveliness.

In the springtime, quiet watching will soon reveal newts but they are extremely sensitive to vibrations. There are two fairly common species, the common or smooth newt and the palmated newt; a third, the great crested newt, is a magnificent but alas increasingly rare species. If you are the fortunate owner of a garden pond with newts *in situ* you will be able to watch their spring courtship. If you have the pond set in a lawn or paving lie or kneel so that your eyes are close to the surface and choose a position so that reflections are reduced to a minimum. Sooner or later, if you are silent and still, you will see one of the newts walking about and maybe, if he is a male, courting a female with vibrations of his curled tail and animated movement. If he is a palmate newt you can recognize him by the thread-like filament at the end of his tail, whereas the male smooth newt's body is heavily spotted with black and he has a reddish belly. Do not look for newts in the pond after August for by then they will have left for the damp world of grass roots and the airy wetness beneath stones.

Perhaps the greatest delight of a springtime and summer pond is the rich variety of plants, aquatic and moisture-loving, that each year appear in succession, colouring the scene with delicacy and brightness. In the marshy

OPPOSITE:
A few of the underwater creatures to be seen in most ponds: (on the surface, left to right) water measurer; common toad; pond skater; common frog; (under the water, left to right) horse leech; ramshorn snail; dytiscus beetle; dragonfly larva; water scorpion; water boatmen.

WINTER'S WINDOW

That night, in the cold starlight, the north wind drew its icy fingers across the water and by dawn had sealed the pond in ice. A few spears of the yellow flag thrust through and the reeds were unmoving in its grasp. Just a few weeks ago there had been life aplenty here as insects, born of the water, luxuriated in the warm sun. Today a grey hushed silence prevailed. Still clinging to a reed stem, the empty larval case of a dragonfly trembled in the wind, a wistful reminder of the loveliness that had emerged above the flowering water forget-me-nots. Now all life was battened down for the winter, sunk into the mud, shrouded with dead skeletonized leaves; larvae for next season's flight; water spiders silk-sealed in empty water-snail shells and plants holding life-secrets in swollen stems and roots. But the north wind was the passerby: the south wind would return once more to sojourn for the summer and release the vibrant life below, hidden for awhile behind the ice windows of winter.

FIELD-WORK

All the gardening magazines advertise plastic pools and garden pond liners which are easy to install and will provide a wonderful habitat for pond life. Most garden centres have fibre-glass ponds on display and also offer a good range of waterside and aquatic plants.

The number of species that arrive and colonize a pond is truly amazing and you may even find toads and frogs assembling and spawning there. Well-planted and established ponds will have their own populations of water beetles, larvae and, hopefully, a dragonfly flying among the waterside flowers.

Use a small mesh net to trawl through the pond weeds and place your catch in any shallow plastic or metal dish. Your catch may contain newts, dragonflies and other larvae, diving beetles of all kinds, and perhaps a water spider. Having taken a long look at them *return them to the pond*.

SITES TO VISIT

Natural ponds are a disappearing feature of our landscape, as more and more wetland is drained. By careful study of Ordnance Survey maps, ponds or likely situations for them can be found. Farmers and landowners usually give permission for a visit and the County Naturalist Trust will know locations of ponds.

ground at the edge of a natural pond (and indeed streams as well) the lovely marsh marigold or kingcup announces that spring has arrived – its showy, yellow blooms attract all manner of insects. Later in the season great hairy willowherb or codlins-and-cream raises its rose-coloured flowers beside the meadowsweet with its scent of summer. The most evocative plants of this waterside scene are the aromatic pleasures of water mint, in its season, the handsome flowers of the yellow iris or flag and the tiny blue beauty of water forget-me-nots. This lovely little flower is worth a closer look with a hand-lens. Pond-watching is undoubtedly a particularly absorbing pastime.

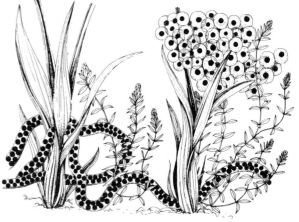

In spring, frog spawn (above) is becoming more rare, but toad spawn still fills small ponds and rain-filled ditches.

THROUGH THE MEADOWS

The scarlet-dotted fly knows nothing of the names of the grasses
that grow here, where the sward nears the sea, and thinking of him
I have decided not to wilfully seek to learn any more of their names
either. I will sit here on the turf and the scarlet-dotted flies shall
pass over me, as if I too were but a grass. I will not think, I will be
unconscious, I will live.

RICHARD JEFFERIES: *Field and Hedgerow* (1889)

Spend awhile enjoying the delicate
natural beauty of summer grasses:
(left to right) perennial ryegrass;
meadow foxtail; timothy; hairy
brome; cocksfoot; yorkshire fog.

Crane fly (above) has a
pair of wings reduced to
'drumsticks' (halteres)
which act as gyroscopic
stabilizers. It shares this
grass stem with a
harvestman.

The summer grasses rise tall, a jungle, fragile, swaying in the breeze, a beautiful, restful environment to explore. If you come upon a hay-field before the time of cutting, or better still an old meadow that has not known the plough for several score years, or wild open downland, sit among the flowers and take a closer look. The variety of grasses and the flowers that grow among them will provide food for thought for many a day.

Names of plants and animals can prove to be a problem, especially when they have no descriptive English name and the Latin tag is long and tongue twisting. The importance of names can so easily be over-rated and at times it can stand between the watcher and the watched, for the feeling of ignorance – the lack of knowledge that one feels to be so essential – assumes undue importance. The real fun, the essence of looking at an insect at work or the colour and form of a flower is a purely visual act, with sound and possibly touch and scent acting as valuable supplements. There are no name plates to be seen in nature. But there are signs to be read, such as colour, form, design and action which tell stories quite beyond the capacity of an advertising hoarding. But like so-called 'good advertising' the message is often subliminal.

However, to communicate our observations to others and to distinguish between species or individual plants and animals so that we can catalogue them in our memory filing system, names are helpful. Let names come slowly. If you are sufficiently interested in what you are looking at, you will surely want to know more and then as you go to the reference book the name will be assimilated.

And so to *Phalangium opilio*, named by the great Linnaeus in 1761, known as a harvestman, a creature like a large spider with eight long, spindly legs living in damp herbage along the edge of fields. They are nocturnal, predatory omnivorous, egg-laying spiders and even in daylight if you disturb the under-

growth you will probably see one. They are quite harmless and when threatened have three methods of self-protection: ejecting a nauseous fluid, casting a leg, and 'shamming dead'. Handle them gently and watch them walk through the grass, constantly tapping ahead to test the surface. They grow by moulting their outer skin, but are short lived, most dying at the end of their first year.

If you sit and wait and the day is warm, with the softest of breezes, you will become aware of the murmur from thousands of insects, most intriguing being the songs of

EVENING ENCOUNTER

The rim of the distant hill held the red orbed sun in the gaunt arms of a scots pine as the merest wisp of haze rose from the stream. Leaning on the lichen-crusted gate, I was enjoying the summer-evening scents: sweetness of honeysuckle; water mint crushed into tangy perfume by the bullocks' feet as they drank; and the heady, all pervasive aroma of pollen-laden grass. Soft sounds of flowing water, muted bird song, nearby leaves rustling to the movement of an unseen bird hunting for its supper.

Out of the dimpsy, floating, gliding ghostly white, a barn owl drifted along the margin of the field, its softness born of the subtle hues of evening, yet couched within its feathers hard, sharp talons. Soaring slightly, it hovered and then plummeted into the grass.

It happened too far away to be certain, but most likely the end of a survival struggle between mouse and owl. Mouse and owl, each equipped with senses beyond man's understanding – the little fieldmouse, its huge light-collecting night eyes, radar-dish ears swivelling to detect the faintest sound borne on the darkening air grasshoppers and crickets. Tune in, home in, watch and listen. The songs are usually made by the males and are caused by stridulation, that is rubbing one part of the body against another. To be more precise, the grasshopper rubs the inner surface of its hind legs, which have a row of sharp fine points, against a raised vein on the outside of the leathery forewing, whereas the crickets rub the base of the forewings together. The antennae provide the clue for visual identification: grasshoppers have short stout antennae and crickets long threadlike antennae. If you want to tell the difference between the sexes, look at the tip of the abdomen: in crickets and bush crickets the ovipositor (the female) is usually sickle-shaped and long, but in grasshoppers it is very short and sometimes even partly out of sight within the abdomen. Most of the grasshoppers feed on grasses but the crickets thrive on a very mixed diet of various plants together with succulent leaves, such as dandelion and clover, and a wide variety of insects such as caterpillars, greenfly and other soft forms. In their behaviour, grasshoppers never fight each other, but sort each other out by singing.

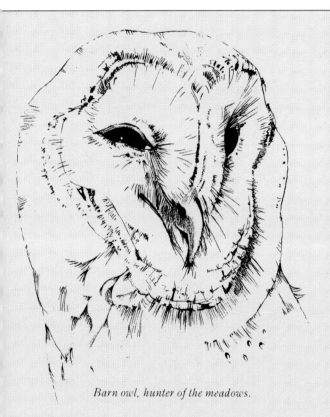

Barn owl, hunter of the meadows.

any predator, for even if detection equipment failed, then sudden explosive leaps and a headlong rush into a root thicket would ensure survival.

But above, in the dusk, the owl hovered, soft feathers soundless, bright round eyes focussed on the tiny animal among the cocksfoot and brome grass. Then the plunge, legs extended, scimitar claws piercing the little prey, and quick death in the jungle grass.

A classic duel. Each equipped for survival, yet the smaller and more numerous mammal inevitably the loser where sheer numbers supplemented the individual skills that ensured the continuance of the species.

My ears were too insensitive to hear the last breathing squeak and I could only imagine the sudden extinction of sound, touch and light. But my eyes watched as the owl rose and transferred its prey from claw to beak as it flew off back to the nest.

In the silence, moths hovered their night flight, a great green bush-cricket chanted high in the hedge and way above the lanterns of the night were lit. One more scented summer evening to remember.

and fringe of shivering whiskers outspread from the side of its tiny pink nose. Surely a most effective night operator, gnawing seeds under the grassy canopy, ready to freeze into immobility at the merest whisper of danger. Safe one would think from

Many of the females can sing although their song is much quieter and is usually heard when she is ready for mating. The male field cricket has a calling song to attract a female and to establish territory, a courtship song which varies as male and female come closer together, and the male's fighting call – which avoids the physical clash of two males.

One bush cricket you are never likely to confuse is the great green bush cricket – principally because of its large size. It is bright green with a touch of brown along its back and has yellowish legs. Once when riding on a combine harvester harvesting barley I saw dozens of these lovely crickets leaping and flying ahead of the machine, obviously disturbed by the vibration and noise. Fortunately for those interested in crickets they are also found in fields where they hunt and consume quite sizeable insects.

During the summer months, butterflies fly freely over the fields and one or two species are common. They generally occur in fields where their larvae's food plant is abundant. They also tend to favour sloping or level meadows and factors such as prevailing winds, moisture levels and the degree of disturbance are all important considerations.

At all ages 'loose' feathers on thighs distinguish rook (right) from crow.

FIELD-WORK

Making recordings of grasshoppers and crickets can be quite challenging, with its problems of wind and microphone distance, but very rewarding when successful.

Grassland provides many opportunities for close-up photography. You will need a reflex camera with a macro lens and a small tripod is essential. Use a fast transparency film. Approach butterflies and insects very slowly as they are extremely sensitive to movement.

Take a good wildflower book and spend an hour identifying some of your finds. Use a good pocket hand-lens X10 and kneeling down, look at flowers in close-up, examine seeds. Such magnifiers are obtainable from an opticians or from: Griffin & George, Ealing Road, Alperton, Wembley, Mdx HA0 1HJ, and cost from £2.00–£5.00.

Spend a while butterfly watching and identify and watch a few insects visiting the flowers. Collect a few grasses. They make interesting flower displays – unless you suffer from hay-fever. In early autumn set out to find a harvestman, a cricket and two kinds of grasshopper.

Always obtain permission from the landowner and observe the Country Code.

SITES TO VISIT

Since much of our countryside is composed of fields, your options are wide open. By careful observation and knowing the district you may be able to locate an old meadow and this will be most rewarding. Contact the local Naturalist's Trust for information on field areas worth visiting, and always obtain permission from the landowner.

The South Downs
Information: Nature Conservancy Council, Foxhold House, Thornford Road, Crookham Common, Headley, Newbury, Berks RG15 8EL. Chalk flora and insects.

Yorkshire Dales National Park
Write to: Park Committee, Colvend, Hebden Road, Grassington, Skipton, North Yorkshire BD23 5LB. Limestone species.

Local town and tourist information offices usually have a wide range of leaflets on nature trails and reserves.

KEY TO PAGES 82–83
Flowering summer meadows offer a host of butterflies to observe: 1 peacock; 2 marbled white; 3 wall butterfly; 4 common blue; 5 painted lady; 6 small copper; 7 ringlet; 8 red admiral; 9 large skipper; 10 green-veined white; 11 meadow brown; 12 small tortoiseshell; 13 comma; 14 gatekeeper.

ALONG THE HEDGEROW

*The most interesting parts, by far, of published natural history,
are those minute, but most graphic particulars, which have been
gathered by an attentive watching of individual animals.*

PHILIP HENRY GOSSE (1854)

According to where you live, so your definition of a hedge will vary: from tall earth banks surmounted by bushes to lichen-encrusted slate walls; from prickly hawthorn to entwined beech; and the dry-stone structures of the uplands. However, they do have one factor in common, a place that provides shelter and home for a rich variety of plants and animals. The life they harbour will also be influenced by the adjacent land use. For instance, you may well have watched magpies standing on the back of a sheep plucking its wool for a nest; or perhaps seen a flock of fieldfares feasting on rowan berries in a tree with roots fast in a bouldered hedge bank, when snow covers the moors. So, fortunately, your exploration of a hedge offers tremendous variety, and it can begin almost anywhere.

One of your first observations may well be the close relationship between creatures and plants. While blackbirds solely use the hedge as a nesting place, linnets may visit to feed on the grass seeds; thrushes come for snails in the hedge bottom; owls hunt close by on lookout for small mammals living there and sparrow hawks prey on the small birds; while mistle thrushes come for the berries.

One of the commonest birds of the hedgerow is the aptly named hedge sparrow or dunnock, and watching one of these solitary and rather skulking birds is a real test of your observational skill. In some ways it resembles a slim house sparrow with a much more slender bill. You will find it often, hopping around in the undergrowth, or making short flights before settling into cover again. It may well disclose its presence by an insistent, shrill yet faint 'tseep, tseep' uttered from deep in cover. It is a little bird often parasitized by the cuckoo. The female cuckoo does not change from one host species to another and so in this instance is always a dunnock-cuckoo, which must only lay in a nest where the dunnock's clutch is incomplete, for the cuckoo cannot lay when the host is incubating – for obvious reasons. The cuckoo will often spend much of the day searching for a nest and having located one she will wait for the owners to leave it for a short while. In an amazing feat of adaptation the cuckoo's egg is already partly incubated when it is laid and this ensures it will hatch before the unfortunate dunnock's eggs. The rest of the story is one of considerable struggle for the dunnock to find the enormous quantity of food for its vastly overgrown visitor. However, hedgerows provide plenty of caterpillars both for the dunnock and its parasite.

In general, the birds that are found in any particular hedgerow depend to a large extent on the adjacent land – whether it is arable, meadow, woodland or moor for such habitats obviously overlap, especially where feeding is concerned. With over five million chaffinches in Britain you should be able to find the nest of one somewhere along the hedgerow. It is a very beautiful and neat nest of twined grasses and ploughed up roots, with the outside covered with lichens gathered from nearby tree bark or stone walls. May is the best time to search. Mistle thrushes build higher and their nest is a much stronger structure of grass, roots and moss, supported with mud and with a dry grass lining. You will find the nest early in March, but the bird will be seen and heard singing its loud song soon after Christmas, probably from a bare branch high in a hedgerow tree.

Outside the breeding season watch the mixed flocks of small birds and try to sort out those 'little brown birds' for there will be bramblings, greenfinches, sparrows, yellowhammers and chaffinches all flying and feeding together.

By way of slight deviation, why not try to date the hedge? A theory propounded by M D Hooper in 1970 is based on a simple formula. First count the number of species in a 30yd (27m) stretch. The age of the hedge = 110 × number of species + 30 years. But first it is advisable to record the number of shrubs in twelve or more hedges that can be dated by documents (your county records office can often help). Then you pace out a 30yd (27m) section of the hedge, chosen at random, and record from one side only the number of species of established shrubs and trees growing there. Should this idea be of particular interest there is a great deal more information in number fifty-eight Collins 'New Naturalist Series': *Hedges* by Pollard, Hooper and Moore.

In spring and early summer the froth called cuckoo-spit is easy to find on a variety of hedgerow plants. Take a closer look, it is quite clean and harmless, despite its unpleasant name-association. Inside the bubble-foam you will discover a little insect nymph called a frog hopper, it is well covered by the camouflage effect of the bubbles, whose moisture also saves them from desiccation. The frothing is caused by the nymph discharging air from breathing through a special valve that places it in contact with fluid issuing from its body – rather like a bubble-gun. Mixed with the froth is a substance from a gland that

Secret of the cuckoo-spit.

A fledgling cuckoo provides a feeding problem for the little dunnock.

The delicate beauty of an emerging sycamore shoot.

Signs of spring: bloody-nose beetle, primroses and celandines.

enables the bubbles to survive the onslaught of rain. These nymphs are gathered by a solitary wasp, which stores them as food in its larva's cell. A good example of hedgerow interdependence.

On a sunny spring day, what better farewell to winter than to see an orange tip butterfly flitting along the hedgerow and to know that summer is really on its way. In May, July and August the wall butterfly will be found on most warm sunny days and those seen flying in May have come out from hibernation, having emerged as adults and flown for a short time at the end of the previous summer. Another butterfly that enjoys basking on leaves in a sheltered part of the hedge is the hedge brown which has another attractive name, the gatekeeper. They seem to be attracted to the flowers of bramble and after supping the nectar, sunbathe on its leaves. By the time the white deadnettle is in flower you will be able to watch queen bumble bees feeding among the flowers, and even into April when the bluebells bloom a few will still be busy.

Watch them as they hover into the grasses to alight and crawl down the leaves searching for a possible nest site, for many of them have not yet established their nests. They are trying to find an old mouse nest with its finely nibbled hay that exactly suits their requirements. Within it the colony will eventually develop during the long summer days.

Hedgerows present a living calendar for any observer who watches the flowers as the year rolls by. The celandine is often the first to bloom at the road's edge, but its golden suns too often are splashed brown with mud.

Often living in close association with this plant and the goosefoot is a large beetle known as the bloody-nose beetle. Its name originates from its habit of discharging an irritant, poisonous fluid from its joints, whenever touched or threatened. But on a sunny spring day its blue-black colour makes it a most conspicuous insect.

'After sunset, the fragrance of honeysuckle is almost too much'. (Hudson)

It is not too long before the sweet fragrance of violets will lead you to the shy flowers nestling among the springing grass in late February. By March the goosefoot, with its prickly stems, is struggling upwards to the flower buds of blackthorn that, viewed from a distance in April, seems to hold a cover of snow among its spines.

Then, as the warmth of the sun penetrates the hedge bottom, sunbursts of dandelions illuminate the grass. Eagerly the stitchwort climbs into the bright light flashing its white stars, and the hedgerow sycamore is breaking into leaf. Suddenly the flowering has turned the hedge into a riot of colour as catkins shake their pollen down over the primroses with their pin-eyed and thrum-eyed blooms. Red campions tower over the shepherd crooks of bracken unfurling and then, suddenly tall, white umbrella flowers are abundant and the cow parsley is overshadowed by giant hogweed. Now the perfume of summer is released from the very earth and perhaps the sweetest of all is the honeysuckle, the flower described by W H Hudson in 1903 thus:

> After sunset the fragrance of the honeysuckle is almost too much; standing near the blossom-laden hedge when there is no wind to dissipate the odour, there is a heaviness in it which makes it like some delicious honeyed liquor which we are drinking in.

The long summer days are a very special time to be out in the country. After a day of sunlight as the dusk spreads over the fields, the hedgerow gives up its scented secrets and the moths come out to sip the nectar, crickets call from the shadowed foliage, a late robin scolds a little owl that alighted on a gatepost, and then it is quiet and still and you are at one with the environment.

But as summer's warmth gives way to shortening days more flowers brighten the hedgerow – St John's-wort, valerian and musk mallow and a host of others that appear at this time. And from this flowering come the fruits and a rich harvest for man and birds. By late autumn much of the plant growth has died down and among the damp and rotting vegetation all manner of fungi are found, which, lacking the chlorophyll to make their

CELANDINE AND BULLDOZER

The dawn chorus had long since faded as the bulldozer started up. Its mechanical roar sent a blackbird screaming alarm from its nest in the ivy that grew over the stump of a dead elm. Within minutes two lorries arrived and the bulldozer clamped its shiny jaws to take the first bite out of the hedge. For machinery had come to remove it; it was deemed necessary that traffic should proceed a little faster through the lane. This was the hedge where years ago my grandmother had shown me where the pignuts grew among the celandines and on one memorable afternoon parted the grasses in the hedge bottom to reveal the wonder of a yellowhammer's nest. Now the very earth was ripped out to make way for tarmac. No more would that lane hear the 'Little bit of bread and no cheese' song of the yellowhammer descendants of that nest. An hour or so later an old oak bowed to the tearing chain saw. That oak had survived due to the hedger's caring trimming when it was a mere seedling a century ago – no longer would it provide acorns for hungry jays and in the still night no longer would the tawny owl proclaim his territory from its canopy.

Later that day I walked along the torn and shattered remnants of the flattened hedge where celandines had graced so many a spring. Today, yellowhammer, tawny owl, blackbird, pignuts, oak, ivy and golden celandines were gone and the community down the road had gained a few seconds of time for each passing car.

Then I came upon a golden gleam in the ruptured soil; delicate petals torn and leaves crushed, the celandine bore mute testimony to time's advance.

Pignut (white clusters); giant valerian (pink clusters); bindweed (white trumpet); bramble.

own food, soak up the green plants' manufactured foods now being released back into the soil. As you continue to explore a hedgerow you will be constantly surprised, and you will come to appreciate the interdependence of the plants and animals that share its ever-changing environment.

FIELD-WORK

Make a point of visiting a particular hedgerow at various intervals through the year. In this way you will get to know the sequence of events and the species that live there. Most naturalists keep a diary of observations, which can be brief or extended as you choose. If you can draw, a sketch will be worth a hundred words. If you can park your car in a conveniently quiet layby, it makes an excellent hide to observe the birds. Try dating a hedge and perhaps follow this up with some enquiries at your local records office or reference library.

Become acquainted with the monthly succession of flowers and try to identify some of them. If you walk along a hedge, stop every few yards, wait and be very still, and then look more closely, really closely. In spring try to recognize birds from their songs and plants from their early growth. In summer identify the flowers and bushes and take a close look at some of the smaller flowers and seeds with a hand-lens. If you happen to go blackberrying you will have a wonderful opportunity to see the great variety of insects that live in the hedge, including those that mine their way between the top and lower surface of the blackberry leaves. In autumn check out all the berries, fruits, lichens, fungi and mosses.

SITES TO VISIT

Despite a great deal of destruction there are still thousands of miles of hedges around our countryside. Their rich variety of structure and species ensures a wealth of sites to observe throughout the year. While those contiguous to highways are free to explore (if perhaps a little dangerous and polluted from traffic) those situated on private property should be respected and permission sought before entering the land.

Autumn fruits: rosehips; honeysuckle; spindle; white bryony; sloe.

91

AROUND THE WOODS

*The bird upon the tree utters the meaning of the wind – a voice of
the grass and wild flower, words of the green leaf; they speak
through that slender tone.*

RICHARD JEFFERIES

The rich diversity of woodland in our countryside and its proximity to most of us offers
wonderful opportunities for getting close to
nature. The moment of walking into a wood
somehow seems to shut the door on the noisy
world we live in and while the silence can be
well-nigh tangible, there are sounds galore,
and for the keen observer, very much to see.

For a very special treat, set the alarm to an
hour before sunrise one May morning and go
to a local deciduous or mixed woodland to
listen to the dawn chorus. Under the stars the
wood is darkly shadowed, but soon the bright
sparkling above the canopy fades a little and
one by one the birds awake, and the males
begin to proclaim their territory. The first
singer to greet the dawn is often the blackbird,
followed closely by a song thrush and by the
time the wood pigeon awakes the harsh caw-
ing of a carrion crow announces its presence. A
nearby robin, a distant pheasant and, slowly,
the woodland throng give voice to the light of
a new day. Sad would be the soul not stirred
by such a chorus. By the time the first rays of
light gild the bluebells the very air is vibrant
with the airborne chorus of bird song and the
great quantity of singers illustrates the diversity of birdlife in the wood.

If, later in the day, you want to discover
exactly what is living in the wood, the best
way to enjoy your watching is to make sure
you are the observer. To do this find a
comfortable spot where you can rest your
back against a tree and melt into the surroundings by keeping quite still and very

quiet. Your arrival will have been noticed by
hundreds of eyes and ears for sadly man
presents such a threat to wild creatures that
they immediately hide themselves as soon as a
human appears. So be patient and while you
wait, look around, for there is so much to see.
The fragile opening leaves in shades of green
beyond the imagination, so many that you
will never again think of green as a single
colour; their shapes, and high above, the
tracery of leaf mosaic individual to each tree;
the colours, texture and form of barks from
rugged oak to spiralled sweet chestnut and
lichen-mottled ash. A feast for the eyes.

For a while, as you wait, enjoy the quiet and
sounds so faint they hover on the very edge of
silence. The soft stirring of leaves beyond
number, variations as the breeze strikes the
chords of sharp edge, scallops and sprays; the
somnolent buzz of a queen bumble bee gather-

*In April and May,
queen humble bees can be
watched as they search for a nest site.*

92

ing nectar from a bluebell at your feet; a winter-wearied twig falling into the leafy carpet. Slowly, as we listen, our ears become more sensitive and the hum of wings, as many insects pass to and fro, can be heard. Then one by one the creatures of the wood accept our presence and begin to move around.

The sudden sharp cry of a shrew encountering another among the leaves of the woodland floor; a wren flutters into the depths of honeysuckle and a robin alights on a nearby branch and utters its warning, flashing a flame of red as it bobs and turns. In the distance comes the rapid drumming of a great spotted woodpecker defining its territory, beating its bill down on to a hollow or semi-rotten branch at a speed of twenty times a second. It does not get a headache because its upper jaw has a highly developed muscle which effectively dampens down the shocks and prevents damage to the brain case.

But much closer to where you are sitting, a tree creeper, a little mouse of a bird, runs up a tall oak trunk probing for insects; a woodpecker yodels his laughing call and alights at a nest hole; a chiff-chaff utters his name from a tall ash tree and a squirrel leaps with breathtaking accuracy across sunlit space. Suddenly your heart misses a beat as a wood pigeon claps its wings out of a conifer, followed immediately by the alarm call of a blackbird. What caused the sudden panic we may never know, but suffice to say we are part of the scene and becoming more and more aware of what there is to see and hear.

Springtime in the woods is a magical time with the birds at the peak of their activity, but it is only by staying in one spot for a while that you will begin to see things. By walking about you are advertising your presence, wherever you go. Bearing that in mind, and having visited the woodland at dawn, the next most rewarding time is about an hour before dusk, just about owl-light time in late September. This is probably the best time of the year to

listen to owl calls, especially the tawny owl. Settle down comfortably with a thermos as the light fades and dusk creeps across the wood. A few minutes before it is completely dark you will hear the first hooting as a tawny proclaims its territory from its daytime roost. It is a challenge to neighbouring owls, the long drawn-out hoot echoing through the wood, a beautiful call amplified by the silence. If another claimant happens to be near, then you are in for a feast of sound, almost frightening in its intensity – a 'caterwauling screaming' that is quite spine-chilling if you are unaware of its cause. Owls sometimes dispute in this way for several minutes before silence is followed by one or two quiet 'kewick' calls from the female, letting the male know where she is.

By now you will have become familiar with the territory of a particular tawny owl and if you go back on a frosty winter night, again at dusk, you will again hear the female calling 'kewick' followed by a gentle 'oo-wip', as the male, having caught a small mammal, returns to offer her food. Again, during the breeding season from March onwards you will hear a great deal of 'conversation' between the pair as the male utters a variety of hoots, some of which are flute-like as he brings in food for his mate. This time of the year the female leaves the nest at dusk and gets quite excited, uttering her soft call in anticipation of the coming meal. In June and July the young can be heard from dusk until dawn, persistently calling for food as the parents comb the wood for bank voles and long-tailed fieldmice and worms.

One warm night in late summer, while the owls are busy about their business, try some night-mothing. Use the sugaring technique described in the 'Field-Work' section, and on a good night you will be more than a little surprised at the large number and variety of moths that fly in to sup on the solution you offer. As you inspect your sugar patches with

a torch you may be disappointed by the small number of moths arriving. However, wait for half an hour and try again and you may be in luck. A number of factors increase the likelihood of a good woodland mothing expedition: weather is quite important, but no doubt the presence of other food sources, such as abundant flowers nearby, can affect the number of moths feeding on your patch.

A woodland has much to offer in every season of the year, but it is most beautiful in autumn. On a sunny day, a walk through the colourful scene over the carpet of multi-coloured leaves is wonderfully invigorating. If there is a light wind blowing, the cascading leaves are a riot of shades, crisp and dry underfoot as you rustle through them, with the white delicacy of old man's beard forming arched bowers with the twining stems of honeysuckle and the lichen showing green on fallen twigs. And growing up among the leaves will be a host of fungi in all shapes, sizes and colours, a veritable treasure-trove for an artist or simply a delight to an observer with a little time to spare. Many species are found in very specific habitats, but every autumn there will always be a selection in every wood.

As the year moves on and brings in those bitter easterlies from Siberia, there will come a day or night when the brooding clouds bring blizzard conditions. Go to a wood when the wind dies away and the pale winter sunlight shines, and experience the ethereal beauty of snow and ice in the cold silence beneath the grey trees. There is a sparkle on the holly that no Christmas decorator can match; the splendour of woodland snow, infinitely shadowed and sculptured reveals itself only to those who venture under the trees when the winter blizzard has passed.

FIELD-WORK

To make the sugar solution for a night's mothing, mix about equal quantities of brown sugar, treacle and beer to a sticky liquid. Boil it down until it is the consistency of thick paint. Add a small amount of rum and (if you can get it) a drop or two of essence of jargonelle pears. Paint it on to tree trunks in a patch about 2in (5cm) wide and 12in (30cm) long. Do this to about twenty trees. Visit with a torch every twenty minutes. Do not collect the moths, simply enjoy watching them.

On a spring dawn in May get up early and go out and hear the dawn chorus. Over a period between late September until June go into the wood at dusk and stay awhile to listen to the owl music. In the daytime sit against a tree trunk and watch the birds that come into sight and those squirrels too.

Have you thought about joining Men of the Trees. Write for information to Freepost, Crawley, West Sussex RH10 4ZB or, if you prefer, apply for membership to the Woodland Trust. SAE to Autumn Park, Grantham, Lincs, NG31 6LI.

SITES TO VISIT

There are approximately 2,490,000 acres of woodland in Scotland, 2,150,000 in England and 595,000 in Wales, making a grand total of over 5,250,000 million acres in Great Britain. Of this two thirds is conifer forest and one third broad-leaved. In addition there are 425,000 acres of scrub woodland and felled land awaiting replanting. During the past couple of years the Forestry Commission has restocked approximately 20,000 acres of woodland and the private sector has added some 11,250 acres. Since a single acre of woodland offers endless possibilities you will not need to travel far to find a promising site for observation.

Yarner Wood
NCC Roughmoor, Bishops Hull, Taunton, Somerset TA1 5AA. Managed to conserve examples of Dartmoor woodland habitats. Nature trail and woodland walks. Permit required away from marked walks.

NIGHT-SHIFT

Late evening was seeping into the wood and the trees were becoming grey silhouettes when the sudden alarm call of a blackbird cut through the quietness. Instead of fading, the call persisted as the bird alighted on a branch emerging from a thick cluster of ivy which was liberally interlaced with tendrils of old man's beard. He was joined almost immediately by a robin, which bobbed and bowed with a persistent 'tic-tic'. Quite unperturbed by this show of aggression a thrush continued to sing merrily atop a tall ash nearby. Quickly, the noisy pair were joined by two blue tits and a tree sparrow which also showed extreme excitement and voiced their disapproval of whatever was hidden in the thicket. Every so often the mob would change perches, only to alight and carry on the urgent cacophony of calls.

Something was hidden among those leaves so I watched and waited, for by now a chaffinch had joined in. Hopping, posturing, wing flipping and screaming, the little birds moved in closer and then suddenly the whole gamut of behaviour escalated as a tawny owl swept out of hiding pursued by the motley mobbing throng. It flapped gracefully away through the trees as one by one the little birds abandoned the chase.

Quietness descended on the wood. A distant cuckoo called and, as the thrush song died away, only the small call of the robin came from a nearby holly bush. But as I left the shelter of the trees a tawny owl hooted. The night-shift was out and about.

Kingley Vale
NCC 'Zealds', Church Street, Wye, Ashford, Kent TN25 5BW. Finest natural yew forest in Europe. Summer manned display/information centre open Sundays, plus nature trail. Permit required for access to Bow Hill.

Coedydd Maentwrog
NCC Plas Penrhos, Ffordd Penrhos, Bangor, Gwynedd LL57 2LQ. Nature trail with leaflet.

Abernethy Forest/Glen Tanar
Head Warden NNR Speyside Reserves, Ben Avon, East Terrace, Kingussie, Inverness-shire PH21 1JS. Large surviving native pinewood, juniper, birch. Dell Wood has capercaillie, Scottish crossbill and crested tit. Red and roe deer, red squirrels and fox.

Beinn Eighe
Information NNR Reserve Warden, 'Ialtag', Anacaun Field Station, Kinlockewe, Ross-shire IV22 2PD. Biosphere Reserve 1976 (UNESCO) award 'European Diploma' Council of Europe 1983. Pine martens, ptarmigan and golden eagle. Visitor centre and nature trails.

Write also for *Reserves Visiting*, The Lodge, Sandy, Bedfordshire SG19 2DL.

OVERLEAF:
Autumn fungi: (top row, left to right) shaggy ink cap; death cap; (middle row, left to right) fly agaric; puff ball; boletus; (bottom row, left to right) morel; parasol; chanterelle.

UNDER THE OAK TREE

From the oak, green caterpillars slide down threads of their own
making to the bushes below, but they are running a terrible risk.
For a pair of whitethroats or 'nettle-creepers' are on the watch, and
seize the green creeping things crossways in their beaks.

RICHARD JEFFERIES

On a sunny day it is a pleasant, relaxing way to spend an hour sitting under or near a tree, especially an oak. Among its massive branches and canopy of leaves live or visit a vast community of small creatures, from minute gall wasps that could fly through the eye of a needle to a large bird such as a jay or buzzard. Their lives are interwoven, their lifestyle ideally suited to life among the wind-tossed leaves. A community almost hidden, yet there for any naturalist to discover.

There are two main kinds of oak, the first, the durmast oak, has acorns borne directly on the twigs and its leaves are stalked and have a tapered base. The second, the pedunculate oak, is recognized from its acorns borne on stalks but its leaves are without stalks and have small lobes at their base.

A single oak tree has more than enough living creatures to give any observer of natural history endless days of pleasure, whether it be an isolated, solitary tree or a member of a woodland community. Those pleasures of discovery in a single oak slowly build from the unknown into a rich fund of familiar knowledge that reveals relationships, facets of behaviour, and connections almost as diverse as the leaves on the tree. And even on a small oak about 10in (10cm) in trunk diameter there are well over 12,000 leaves which represent a leaf area of over 18 square metres. The Biological Flora lists 227 species of fauna associated with oaks, far richer than any other tree.

The jay is a noisy, garrulous bird that visits the oak at acorn time. Resplendent in colourful plumage, this member of the crow family is responsible for much of the natural regeneration of oak trees and it is fascinating to watch them feeding when the acorns are ripe. The bird pulls off as many as five acorns and gulps them down to store in its oesophagus and then plucks another one to carry in its beak. It then flies a short distance from the tree, regurgitates and 'plants' them underground as winter food store. Not being able to recall exactly where each is buried, many survive and germinate. Many of these young seedlings, by the following summer, are a few centimetres tall and the jays dig down to nip off the two seed leaves (cotyledons). They do this without causing damage to the young oak, which continues to grow and thrive. It has been said that the jay is the only means whereby oaks can colonize uphill, for the naturally falling acorn will always roll down a slope.

The first animals you see visiting the oak will probably be titmice, the most common of which is the blue tit. This little bird arranges its nesting time and number of eggs to coincide with the population explosion of caterpillars. How does the blue tit know that sort of information in advance? Its nestlings' development synchronizes with the peak of the oak caterpillar population explosion. With a pair of binoculars it is possible to watch the feeding technique as the tit inspects under and around the leaves.

Blue tit parents collect well over sixty-five caterpillars for each nestling per day.

that walk with a looping action as they draw their hind feet up to their front legs and form a loop before extending the front end out again. Loopers have three pairs of front walking legs and two pairs at the rear end and feet with fleshy soles for gripping. The 'typical' caterpillar has three pairs of walking legs, four pairs along the abdomen and one pair of soft soles at the rear. If you are fortunate you may see a looper hanging on the end of a gossamer thread which it has discharged from its mouth as it fell off a leaf. It is a very useful survival tactic that enables it to climb back to the leaf by gripping its own life-line.

Most of the caterpillars are masters of camouflage and none more difficult to see than those whose bodies are equipped with bumps shaped like buds and stem bases and which stretch outwards from a twig at an angle, exactly like a small twig. Such perfection of form enables a caterpillar to escape being taken by such sharp-eyed predators as blue tits. In addition to this close resemblance to a twig it is essential for the caterpillar to remain absolutely still because any movement may well be detected; so countless caterpillars feed by night while the daylight predators are asleep. (If you can obtain a copy of *Curious Naturalists* by Niko Tinbergen you will be enthralled by the activities of a small party of naturalists who worked with him, principally studying the art of camouflage.)

Among the insects that live in the oak are some extremely beautiful lacewings – slender-bodied with marvellous gauzy wings and iridescent green bodies and eyes of gleaming gold. Their larvae stalk among the leaves, their bodies hidden under a mass of debris, seeking aphids which they seize in pincer-like jaws.

If perchance you have chosen an oak tree in a woodland where wood ants live then there will be all sorts of mayhem to watch. If they are using your tree as a food provider take a closer look as they crawl up and down the

To see a selection of the 220 odd living forms in your chosen oak, you will need to employ a simple technique. Hold an open and inverted umbrella under a group of oak branches and give the bough a very smart tap with your hand. This dislodges most of the occupants which then fall into the brolly and can be examined in a small transparent box. Use a hand-lens to study the very small creatures such as tiny spiders, weevils and beetles. Instead of an umbrella you may prefer a newspaper or make a simple cloth tray on a tied frame of bamboo. *Conservation note*: Do not carry out this procedure to excess and always return the living creatures to the oak leaves, which are their homes.

In the summer months you may well be surprised at the variety of caterpillars you find. Some will be 'loopers', that is caterpillars bark. Those small ants climb into the highest branches of the oak and hunt far and wide among the foliage and in the warm days of summer they sup the honeydew. To ensure plentiful supplies of this sweet, energy-giving food they actually farm the aphids by carrying them from a crowded area to a less busy place. They do this because aphids suck the sap from the oak and the ants want to ensure that there is plenty available, with not too many heavy drinkers in one spot. This sap is rather thick so aphids eject saliva into the plant before sucking out the pre-digested fluid. The ants then milk the aphids by stroking them with their antennae, supping up the secreted drops and carrying them back to the nest. When there is a population explosion of aphids they give off more honeydew than the ants can cope with and you will find most of the leaves of the tree are quite sticky with the substance, having dropped from the little insects.

But wood ants also get their meal supply from the oak and catch all manner of insects in the process. You will see single ants carrying small larvae in their jaws, and even small beetles and flies can be taken. Frequently three or four ants will be seen crawling rather haphazardly down the trunk holding a large caterpillar between them. On one occasion I was watching a tree trunk when a red underwing moth alighted on the bark. Within less than half a minute two ants literally leapt on it and all three fell to the ground where others joined in. Finally the moth was dragged over the leaves towards the nest, manoeuvered by six ants. How they catch wasps, I can only guess: perhaps the wasp alights to drink the honeydew and is set upon by the red throng. If you happen to be passing a wood ants' nest before the sun is shining on it, you will see thousands of ants huddled together in a writhing mass on top of the nest, awaiting the

Feathered conservationist: the jay enables oak trees to colonize uphill, *despite the tendency of acorns to roll* down the slope.

An upland oak's buds in early May.

*Search for marble galls
caused by a tiny gall wasp;
there will also be currant galls,
and many other kinds.*

Look for oak catkins in May.

*English or pedunculate oak has acorns on long stalks whereas
durmast oak acorns are stalkless.*

SCENT OF SPRING

February is a month of two faces: one looking back on cold winter past, the other forward to summer's warmth. It is during this month, although every so often we have to wait until March, that there comes a day when we know that spring has come again. There is an indefinable scent that emanates from the very soil itself, the scent of sap rising through innumerable small grass stems; sap coursing beneath the bark of countless trees. The whole realm of nature is responding to the subtle rhythm of seasonal change induced by growing day-length and sunlight on the tired, winter-weary soil. There is a buoyant feeling in the air and we know the countryside is awakening. The shining celandine, the first dandelion, a tattered-winged tortoiseshell butterfly roused from hibernation, a cluster of elder leaves, each tells the unfolding story; shy violets beneath the oak, perfume the breeze that bears winter away. Not for two more months will the oak-buds burst open and release their catkin cascades to dance to the song of May, but today we know with certainty that spring is not too far away.

sun's warmth to set them off on another day.

Living in this leafy world is a highly acrobatic beetle which, although inconspicuous in appearance, is a fascinating performer. If you find one when you are tree beating it will almost certainly fall on to its back, legs in air, and stay motionless. Wait a while and you will hear it suddenly give a click and see it leap several centimetres into the air, alight and scuttle away to cover. Hence the common name click beetle or skipjack. It is about 2cm long, brownish and narrow bodied, but a contender for the high jump in the insect Olympics.

Most of us are familiar with oak apples, although what many refer to by that name are in fact oak marble galls – clusters of brown marble-sized growths on the twigs of the oak. The true oak apple galls are much larger, rosy-pink when young, turning brown later and quite irregular in shape. Oak trees produce innumerable galls, the majority formed by the activities of insects. For instance, a gall-insect may lay an egg in the leaf bud which results in a stimulus that causes the bud to grow into an abnormal shape, meanwhile housing the larvae of the insect. Many of these galls have fascinating and intricate life histories and one research worker observed hundreds of collected galls from which over twelve thousand females emerged and not one, single male! If you cut into a marble gall you will find the tiny grubs, but if there are small holes in the skin the adult gall wasps have emerged. A few woodland birds know there is food within the gall and you will find many that have been broken apart as they searched for the larvae hidden within.

On the underside of oak leaves from July onwards, clusters of fifty or more common spangle galls can be found. They are a greenish colour, and covered in small reddish hairs. Their unique story is worth relating. In September the galls fall away from the leaf into the leaf-litter at the base of the tree, carrying the tiny larva which will overwinter within. Some time during April, dependent on weather, a wingless female gall wasp emerges from each one. They crawl up the trunk and lay their eggs among the oak catkins which appear in May in the berry-like galls that look exactly like red currants. The insects emerging from these galls are the bisexual generation which lay their eggs on the underside of the leaves – and so the cycle continues. (See Collins 'New Naturalist' *Insect Natural History* by A D Imms. It is enthusiastically written by a wonderfully keen and highly qualified observer.)

A large and attractively coloured beetle that occasionally feeds on oak is the common cockchafer, with its handsome chestnut-brown wing cases and black and white belly. They come out of hiding at dusk and fly around, making a loud buzzing noise. But like many of the insects that spend time on the oak, you have to search for them, so be patient, persistent and not too disappointed if you make the acquaintance of only a few species on your first visit. Getting to know the creatures, and their fascinating life histories, that live on a particular kind of tree is a rewarding pastime.

FIELD-WORK

Select a particular oak tree, either a solitary one, or one that is part of a woodland community, and observe it over as long a period as possible. Try recording, in diary form, all you see through the seasons. Do a little tree beating and examine your 'catch', but afterwards return them to the leaves. Collect some marble galls in late August and keep them in a plastic container covered with some nylon from an old pair of tights. Some time during September or October you should be able to see the tiny gall wasps when they emerge. Be sure that the galls you collect do not have small holes in them. In May and June search for currant galls among the oak catkins; in late summer look on the underside of oak leaves for spangle galls. Spend a while by your oak and watch for bird visitors and try to discover why they have come to the tree. Do some sugaring (see page 96).

By searching and scraping among the leaves and soil under the oak you may find the pupae of some of the caterpillars that lived in the tree. They can be kept in a plastic container with some damp, *not wet*, sterile peat and a cover of nylon mesh. Keep in a shaded, cool place and examine regularly. Try to identify the emergent moths and then release them.

In autumn, watch the jays as they feed on the acorns.

SITES TO VISIT

Countryside and parkland throughout most of the British Isles supports large numbers of oak trees, so look around for a tree that is large, in good growth condition and easily accessible. Make sure it is either a durmast or pedunculate oak and not one of the ornamental oaks planted for decoration.

Look for the rich variety of plants growing on the oak; the polypody fern is a common one.

UP AND OVER THE MOORS

Moving up the sweet short turf, at every step my heart seemed to obtain a wider horizon of feeling; with every inhalation of rich pure air, a deeper desire. The very light of the sun was whiter and more brilliant here.

RICHARD JEFFERIES

The richly varied uplands of our country are wonderful places to escape. Landscapes can be placid and inviting on a summer's day and cold and forbidding on a winter's night; in snow or blizzard conditions they can be terrifying. Perhaps it is this ever-changing nature of the environment that is a large part of their appeal, but primarily it is those wide open spaces and the silence that draws us back again and again. And solitude is a rare commodity today, but it can be experienced among the high rocks and wind-pruned bracken where larks sing in vast open skyscapes and where we come, perhaps closest, to a primeval environment. It is a wilderness, still largely untouched by people, for some of the last remote and really wild places are to be found on the moors and among the mountains where some wildlife still ranges free and comparatively undisturbed. Here are places where you can park your car and set off through the bracken, ling and heather to watch badgers and foxes, enjoy the flight of ravens and buzzards, eagles and deer.

The high places exist in various bands, from the arctic-alpine zone down to upland grassland – it is beyond the scope of this introduction to describe them all in detail. (For the reader keen to experience the background to wilderness there are four books by Mike Tomkies who lived among wildcats, owls, foxes and pine martens and who watched and studied golden eagles with the single-minded determination of a perceptive field naturalist of quite indomitable courage. The books are *A Last Wild Place, Out of the Wild, On Wing and Wild Water* and *Wildcat Haven* published by Jonathan Cape Ltd.)

Most of these high areas are very wet places with very high rainfall, and one of the plants you may come across in soft boggy ground is the sundew. It is an insectivorous plant which obtains its nourishment from flies and small insects it catches on its sticky leaves. The leaves have large numbers of sticky red hairs which secrete a liquid which attracts insects, but as soon as the insect alights it finds itself stuck fast and surrounded by a slowly closing network of hair. These curve inwards like tentacles, entrapping the insect and digesting

The sundew is a plant trap for unsuspecting insects.

OPPOSITE:
A sight well worth waiting for; a wary badger.

its body. It is small plant, perhaps 3–5in (8–13cm) in diameter with its rosette of leaves quite close to the ground, so you will have to look closely for it.

Another interesting plant is the dodder. It is parasitic, often on gorse. Your first sighting is likely to be of a coiled network of reddish fibres, almost as if someone had draped a tangled fish net over the bush. But examined closely small pinkish-white flowers will be seen from July to September. As a seedling this plant reaches upwards in twisted coils in an effort to contact the future host plant. As soon as it establishes this contact it twines around the stems (always anticlockwise) and begins to ensnare its host in a straggling mass of stems. If you look very closely you will see that the dodder sends out outgrowths from these stems which penetrate into the host plant and feed on the sap from it. It becomes completely dependent on its host and has no root system in the soil below. A successful parasite and an interesting plant to search for, especially on heaths and downland in England and Wales.

Another plant to look out for is cotton grass, which is easily recognized by its white seed heads looking like light tufts of cotton wool made up of many cottony hairs. They grow in wet boggy ground and are a warning to all walkers to keep clear – a useful sign of where it is unsafe to walk. Although commonly called cotton grass, it is in fact a sedge. And how do you recognize a sedge? Well at first glance it is a little like a grass, but sedges have triangular stems with their flowers in spikelets at the top of the plant. You could confuse a sedge with a rush, but the rush has round, pithy or hollow stems with the flower cluster appearing to be on the side of the stem. Both grow in damp and marshy habitats.

There are three birds you will almost certainly want to find: golden plover, meadow pipit and wheatear. In the breeding season the golden plover favours upland moors where there is plenty of short grass and stunted heather among which it nests in a small depression in the ground. The meadow pipit nests in tussocks or heather clumps and is quite commonly parasitized by the cuckoo. In many places where these pipits are numerous, cuckoos seem to gather, and I once watched four cuckoos working an area the size of a football pitch on some moorland which had large patches of gorse among granite stone walls. In such circumstances as many as ten percent of the meadow pipit nests will fall prey to the cuckoo.

The wheatear tends to be found on bare hillsides and stony mountain tops, often quite barren. Unlike the meadow pipit it is a summer migrant from tropical Africa and all too often it too has to spend much of the summer feeding a cuckoo usurper. Although the nest is often well concealed in a rocky crevice, in a space between stones, in a dry stone wall or even in a hollow receptacle like an old tin, the cuckoo is a good observer. It hides, watches and waits and having pinpointed the nest site by watching the movements of the wheatear, bides its time and then when the occupant has laid its eggs and is away feeding, the cuckoo strikes. In a matter of a few seconds the cuckoo will pick out an egg in its beak and lay one in its place, an egg that is coloured remarkably like the pale blue eggs of the wheatear.

If you are strolling through the bracken and hear a sharp 'tic-tic' often repeated and coming from a small bird perched atop a gorse bush, then you are probably in sight of a whinchat, or perhaps a stonechat. If you want to sort the two out, go to a good identification book because it can be a problem for a beginner. Since the stonechat is more often found near coasts, the bird is more likely to be a whinchat. But as with all problems of identification it does help if you have either a notebook in which to jot down some of the bird's outstanding features, or a sketch pad on which to draw the same. You do not need to be a skilled bird illustrator – simply record what *you* noticed and then, when you get home, or perhaps are sitting among the heather with your bird book, you can begin to get things clear in your mind.

Because they are at the end of the food chain, buzzards are susceptible to the effects of pesticides and poisons.

In the silence of the moors, the mewing call of the buzzard is very much part of the scene and it is a peaceful pastime to relax and watch one, or a pair, circling in the sky. You can watch as they flex and tilt their rounded wings ever so slightly as they ride the thermals, gliding around in wide soaring flight, often rising to a very considerable height and at times disappearing from sight in the clouds.

A bird whose far carrying croak is evocative of all wild places is the jet-black raven – a majestic bird that nests in very inaccessible places such as on ledges beneath overhanging rocks and in the clefts between cliff-side rocks among tors and mountains. Somehow ravens have learned to build their nests in places that only the most experienced of climbers can reach. Perhaps with the modern approach to conservation and the almost total decline in egg-collecting, the raven population will begin to increase.

Autumn, when the berries are ripe on the rowans, is the time to watch a flock of fieldfares alighting on a tree to feed. They are

bold, busy birds and quite noisy. They are sometimes seen in the neighbourhood of isolated farms, but they do need berries – so look for a suitable place with plenty of berries, wait and watch and you may well be rewarded.

Badgers are delightful animals which, for the keen observer, can offer endless hours of pleasure, provided a few very simple rules are obeyed. Firstly, except in really wild undisturbed areas where badgers occasionally come out in summer sunlight with their cubs, they are mostly active from dusk onwards. If you intend to go badger-watching, having found a sett, visit it in the daylight and look closely at the various holes. Some will obviously be unused, with grass or even a flowering plant growing amidst the old earth. The used openings will probably have freshly excavated soil heaps and plenty of signs of footprints and obvious activity; trackways leading out from the hole are another indication. Having had a good look around and found more than one suitable observation point, do not revisit the site for at least a day, so that your scent will

Birds to look for during a moorland walk: (top row, left to right) wheatear; female stonechat; female whinchat; male whinchat; (bottom row, left to right) skylark; male stonechat; meadow pipit.

J. Netley.

dissipate. The reason for locating more than one observation point is so that you may choose one *downwind* from the hole when you arrive. Also make sure the observation point has no bush in the way of clear vision. On arrival, get there half an hour before dusk and make yourself comfortable, it is astonishing how muscles and nerve endings respond to an hour's motionless sitting! I prefer to watch badgers without any light at all. Your eyes soon get used to 'darkness' and it is surprising how much can be seen by star- and moonlight.

So, there you are, sitting, waiting and watching. Suddenly in the small dark opening you see a movement. Half a minute passes. Nothing. Then another movement, indistinguishable as an animal, and again stillness and nothing. But patience will be rewarded and the first moment of seeing that black and white head emerge is a never-to-be-forgotten experience. Now, you must be still for the badger has better night sight than you. But it will come right out and usually begin scratching. As time passes and the night grows darker, it will be joined by a mate and maybe, if the season is right, by its cubs. You can use a torch with red plastic over the lens, but some badgers are sensitive even to this small light, although one or two have been known to ignore the intrusion.

Foxes can be watched on the moors but they are tricky creatures to get close to; although when they have cubs they will often lay out among bracken in broad daylight. The same rules for watching badgers apply to foxes and they often inhabit and even share parts of a badger's sett. You can tell if foxes are present by the bones and feathers that accumulate in the area and, by their freshness or age, get a rough idea of whether they are still in occupation. My own experience with foxes is not highly successful and I think this is echoed by many naturalists who have not specialized in the species.

On the occasions when I have been able to

LARKSONG

Up here among the summer ling, the windsong was hushed to the very edge of silence beneath limitless sky and sunlight. A raven flew by to its nest on the ledge of the tor; from way down in the valley the call of a cuckoo filtered through the quiet air; a pony whinnied in the newtake down beside the river. It was a morning to relax, a time to free the imagination, to feel the very pulse of the land itself.

And then skylark song cascaded out of the sky. The bird so tiny yet its song emotive with all the pleasure of summer. Surely that little bird was experiencing joy; joy in the freedom of flight released into song; joy for the pure, sweet air and warmth upon its wings. Could notes so perfect for the out-of-doors be anything but an ecstatic release of joy within its buoyant body.

Let technology produce its sonagrams and reduce those wonderful notes to lines on a graph. Analysis has no place here on the high moors. For this is the real world where thoughts range free and the ethereal wonder of larksong can be shared with a bird. We need only to listen; to ponder awhile on the outpouring of song to know with certainty that a skylark experiences joy beyond our understanding.

watch foxes it has usually been due to a chance sighting or from watching a site suggested by a local farmer. Farmers are always good sources of information. A farmer I know is excellent at mimicking the call of a fox. One evening we stood on a hill beside a hedge as one barked in the distance. My farmer friend replied and during the next half hour the fox and farmer 'conversed' as the fox came ever nearer. Finally, the nearby cattle grew restless, all looking in one direction, and then walking warily between them, just visible in the moonlight, came the fox. But it was by now suspicious of the imposter's bark, and it turned and trotted off into the night.

FIELD-WORK

Take a picnic lunch and spend a day in one of the high places you have always wanted to visit, but leave the car in the car-park and walk into the country. Binoculars will be useful for bird-watching, especially if you settle down in a likely place and wait for them to come along. Listen for unusual bird song. Have you ever *really* listened to a lark singing? Relax and enjoy that wonderful song.

Search in wet places for sundew and butterwort, two insectivorous plants *but* beware of the boggy ground, it can be very dangerous. Take a closer look at lichens and set out to identify a few of the more common ones. If you are in a suitable site, try and find some dodder and use a hand-lens for a close-up view.

One evening try some badger-watching and if the first time does not produce results try again, for eventually you will be rewarded.

Take a really close-up look at ling and heather and the yellow gorse. Why not spend a short while discovering the differences between sedges and rushes. Familiarity with plants, like knowing friends, is a wonderful way to enrich your life.

SITES TO VISIT

Cairngorms National Nature Reserve

Between Aviemore in Strathspey and Braemar in Upper Deeside rises the largest tract of mountainous land over 900 metres high in Britain. This is the Cairngorms region, 250 square kilometres of which form the reserve. Rare plants. Deer forest for red deer. Roe deer. Foxes, badgers, wildcats, otter and red squirrel. Golden eagles, capercaillie, black grouse, osprey and peregrine falcon. Further information: D A Gowans (Head Warden), Ben Avon, East Terrace, Kingussie, Inverness-shire PH21 1JS. Tel: Kingussie (05402) 678.

Creag Meagaidh

Information: as Cairngorms. Outstanding mountain reserve. Open moorlands are a hunting ground for peregrine, hen harrier and golden eagle.

Exmoor National Park

426 square kilometres in Devonshire and Somerset. Information: Exmoor House, Dulverton, Somerset TA22 9HL. Tel: Dulverton (0398) 23665. Red deer, beautiful scenery. Stamps for a copy of their excellent newspaper/guide.

North York Moors

Official guide: The Old Vicarage, Helmsley, York YO6 5BP. Tel: Helmsley (0439) 70657. Information on 'Where to Go, Where to Stay, What to See'. Guided walks, events and shows, Heritage coast, activities and Moors Centre.

Y Wyddfa, Snowdon

Regional Officer, NCC Plas Penrhos, Ffordd, Penrhos, Bangor, Gwynedd LL57 2LQ. Wide variety of habitats from oak woods near Llyn Dinas, through the intermediate sheep-walk grasslands, to the main arctic-alpine plant communities of the calcareous cliffs and the windswept sub-arctic heath of the exposed summits at over 915 metres. Two trail guides available.

Dartmoor, Devon

Information: Parke, Haytor Road, Bovey Tracey, Newton Abbot, Devon TQ13 9JQ.

Lake District, Cumbria

Park Centre, Brockhole, Windermere, Cumbria.

OUT IN THE GARDEN

*The hours when the mind is absorbed by beauty are the only hours
when we really live, so that the longer we can stay among these
things so much the more is snatched from inevitable Time.*

RICHARD JEFFERIES

Few environments offer better facilities for observation than a garden, because it is close at hand and very familiar to the observer. It also has the great advantage, from a natural history viewpoint, of being infinitely adaptable to the interests of the gardener. Bird tables, ponds, nesting areas, butterfly and insect plants, soil life and all the visitors that come there from sparrow hawks to cats, foxes and sea-birds can each be encouraged.

Since this is not a gardening manual it would be inappropriate to mention in detail the planning and planting of a garden, except to highlight worthwhile tips. A great bonus for the observer of garden wildlife is the fact that there is ample opportunity to sit and watch. Don't be in too much of a hurry to mow the lawn, you can do that later and a few weeds provide food for birds and insects. But gardens are a natural history enigma, a con-

Acrobats at the bird table: blue tits and great tit (top right).

114

stant compromise between wildness and controlled cultivation, a desire to encourage wildlife and the acceptance of your neighbour's cat and the inevitable conflict between children's vociferous enjoyment and the quiet peace of a nature reserve.

In a quiet garden the birds become familiar with your movements and very soon carry on their natural lives even when you are close to them, so affording wonderful moments to study behaviour. In inclement winter weather greenfinches may well arrive to enjoy the peanuts you put out at the bird table, a habit they seem to have developed since the mid 1960s. In general they prefer larger gardens with plenty of shrub cover. The way they react with blue tits while clinging to a nut feeder is fascinating to watch, especially if you site the food within view of a suitable window. Your kitchen or lounge windows make excell-

ent hides for garden bird-watching providing you sit not too conspicuously near the glass.

After the breeding season the beautiful goldfinch visits gardens, providing there is an abundance of seeds, and I have watched them feasting on the heads of michaelmas daisies as well as in a patch of groundsel. Small flocks of six to fifteen birds will arrive, stay for ten minutes or so and then fly off, sometimes returning about the same time of day for perhaps a week or more. By careful watching it is possible to be prepared for their arrival, and so watch their brief stay more effectively.

Have you ever spent a few minutes listening to starling chatter? They are the most vocal of birds and great imitators of other species. During the past two or three months I have heard a curlew, a green woodpecker and a jay upon the television aerial, each quite accurately mimicked by starlings. One of them has

In winter snow, watch for fieldfare (left) and redwing coming into lowland gardens.

even learned the wild faint call of a distant curlew so perfectly that I found myself looking in the distance for the bird itself. Since song is learned in early life it is just possible that that starling heard a curlew call when it was a youngster learning from its own flock. Birds also develop their own subtle version of the species song and no doubt this helps them to be recognized as individuals. In the autumn it is particularly noticeable how starlings gather, an hour or so before dusk, in small parties on the roof, in a tree or some other high spot. They are waiting to join the main flock *en route* for the roosting site which may be some miles away. They are good timekeepers, check from you own watch, always bearing in mind that a dull, misty or bright afternoon will have its effect in advancing or delaying the time.

On a summer's day, sitting on that deck-chair in the sun, keep your eyes open long enough to enjoy the flight of the swifts. If it is possible that birds experience the emotion of joy, one only has to watch swifts for a while to see plenty of evidence, as they move so effortlessly, screaming over the house-tops. Watch as they skim the house front at 40mph banking and turning, and occasionally falling like a tumbled leaf. Surely your heart will rise a little, earthbound as we are, for these birds spend their entire life on the wing so that mating, feeding and drinking all take place over the roof-tops. At night, when we are asleep, parties of swifts spiral upwards into the evening sky well above 5,000ft (1500m) to sleep on the wing.

In periods of really bad weather, when snow blankets the moors, redwings, fieldfares and redstarts come down to lowland gardens along with many other species. The variety of birds that visit your garden is so great, I can only mention a few species here – you must investigate further.

Insects abound in the garden and providing you can be dissuaded from spraying any of these lethal concoctions over your plants, you will find plenty of interest. Have you ever watched bees visiting your flowers? You might be surprised at the enormous variety, including all those small ant-like bees. One of the problems in bee-watching is deciding the difference between a bee, a wasp and a fly for all too often outward appearance can be most confusing. Some bees look like wasps, and vice versa; some flies look like bees or wasps and vice versa. Sorting them out is part of the fun. One sure way to tell bees and wasps from flies is to recall that flies have only one pair of wings whereas bees and wasps have two pairs. Early in the spring, on a warm, sunny day, you will almost certainly be aware of the loud drone of a flying humble (bumble if you prefer) bee queen. This is the time of year when the warmth awakens the queens and they begin to stoke up on energy-giving nectar. They are large, furry bees, some with their rear clothed in bright-red hair like the red-tailed humble bee, others with a band of brownish-yellow at the tail and called buff-tailed humble bees. There will be many more too. When visiting flowers they are not at all aggressive and you can go in very close to watch them, maybe gathering pollen. The flowers they visit often dust their pollen over the bee's hairy back and this is then brushed off by the bee and pushed into a special pollen basket on the rear legs after being moistened with nectar. If the bee has been busy for some little while you will see these pollen lumps, about the size of a grain of rice and varying in colour according to the flowers they have been visiting. Most bees habitually visit one kind of flower at a time and you can witness this by watching a single bee at work.

This early-season visiting queen is the sole survivor from last year's colony, for towards last autumn she emerged as a 'princess', took flight and mated. Throughout the long, cold, wet winter she hibernated in a dry hole, perhaps somewhere in your garden, storing the life-giving sperm within her body to fertilize the eggs which will found this year's new colony. During the course of the year she may lay anything from a few hundred to a few thousand eggs.

If you are very fortunate and keep on the lookout during June and July you may discover that some of the leaves on your rose bushes have neat holes, the size of a small coin, cut out of them. By waiting and watching you may see the leaf cutter bee arrive and set to work. I have watched one many a time, but always feel a sense of wonder at the skill it shows in biting that circle of leaf, often on swaying bushes, seizing it in her mouth and flying off with it. I have also found them at work on our wistaria. These bees form burrows in the soil, old cob walls, wood and similar sites and in them deposit a few eggs. The burrow is then sealed with these pieces of leaf. It intrigues me why they choose a particular bush, but so far I have found no answers – perhaps you will.

Wasps seem to be everyone's enemy, yet they are quite beautiful insects when studied at close quarters. All you need is an egg-cup of water with plenty of dissolved sugar and a small paint brush. Dip the brush into this liquid and place it in front of you with the drop of sugar solution glistening in the sun. Providing wasps are about, usually in late summer and early autumn, one will soon arrive, alight and begin to suck up the liquid. You may be surprised at how much a single wasp can take aboard and perhaps equally surprised at its beauty of colour and form.

If you have, or know of, a garden with plenty of fuchsia bushes you may well come across the very spectacular caterpillar of the elephant hawk moth. They advertise their presence by practically defoliating the entire bush, but if you want to see them feeding come out after dark in July to September, for they are nocturnal feeders. Fully grown, the caterpillar is up to 3in (8cm) in length, and like

THUNDER FLIGHT OF THE ANTS

Vast towers of cumulus were rising over the town and the air was heavy with the impending August storm when the garden became alive with ants. Triggered by season, atmospheric pressure and signs beyond my understanding they came up out of their dark subterranean tunnels into the hot, bright sunlight. They poured out of cracks in the cement path, through a hole in the crazy paving, out between tiny spaces in the pavement and kerb stones – so many it was beyond comprehension that they had lived so inconspicuously for so long in the garden.

They crawled over the flowerbeds and lawn and up the plant stems, some with frail gossamer wings and others wingless. A busy air of excitement and expectation seemed to fill the air although the turmoil was purely instinctive. It was the marriage flight of the ants.

Here were the males and perfect females endowed with wings, while the wingless workers fidgeted among them. Then from the tops of the plants and the tips of grass stems they took off, flying and rising on the thunder thermals to find each other high in the sky, only the fittest males and females mating. Then the return to earth a few minutes later, the fertilized queens seeking a soil-crack or hole in which to start their nest. Biting off their wings, for their brief hour of freedom was over, one by one they went back into the earth. The marriage flight was over; there was much work to be done.

all the hawk moth caterpillars it has a spike-like tail. If you happen to have a poplar or lime tree in your garden, in early autumn you may find caterpillars of the poplar hawk moth and lime hawk moth. Some time ago when the elm disease destroyed an old elm, we replanted with a lombardy poplar and lime tree. Within five years each tree was host to its respective hawk moth – an excellent example of how to attract wildlife to your garden.

In autumn, when the apples fall, leave a few on the ground. After the starlings and wasps have eaten a few holes in them, the butterflies will arrive. On many occasions I have seen tortoiseshell, peacock, speckled wood, comma and red admirals supping up the nectar from wind-falls. Drawn in by the scent of the juice they form quite an assembly and provide some enjoyable autumn butterfly watching. Whether it is the cooler weather or the effect of the juice I cannot say, but they seem much more 'relaxed' on apples than on flowers and consequently that much easier to observe.

The joy of watching the wildlife of your garden will fill every season with new discoveries. You will become more aware of the hidden beauty to be found there and more receptive to the sounds and all the small clues, until you realize your garden is a nature reserve in miniature.

FIELD-WORK

A great bonus of garden wildlife is the control you have over it. Why not create a butterfly garden by planting valerian (*Valeriana officinalis*), sea thrift (*Armeria maritima*), *Sedum spectabile* with michaelmas daisies (*Aster spp*) and Buddleia (*davidii*). Leave a patch of nettles in the corner for the larvae of small tortoiseshells, peacocks and red admirals to feed on.

Install a small pond, fibre-glass or cement are preferable to those black pond liners.

Bird tables and drinking places will attract birds and suitably placed nest boxes usually become occupied, not always in the first year, but when the birds become used to them.

In the nesting season put tufts of wool, and teased-out fibres, in a conspicuous position so that you can watch the birds fly off with the material. Bundles of long twiggy shrub and hedge prunings pushed into a quiet corner often make a good nest site. But always be aware of the threat from cats and try to position things where they cannot easily climb or jump.

Larvae of the elephant hawk moth may be found on fuchsia bushes in late summer.

IN THE TOWN

The more one studies nature the more one becomes convinced that it is an error to suppose things proceed by a regular rule always applicable everywhere – consequently no observation can be accepted as final.
RICHARD JEFFERIES

In many ways the town seems an unlikely place to watch wildlife, yet there are many plants and animals that have adapted to life among buildings. Foremost are the pigeons. They can be watched as they go about their daily business, for pigeons have lived with man for so long that they have lost all fear of our approach. They have learned a lot about survival among the traffic and it is quite amazing to see them searching for food in a busy shopping street – they know how to avoid disaster to within a hair's breadth as they dice with death among the cars. Much safer, and one feels much more rewarding, would be to feed in the squares and small parks where people pour out breadcrumbs and grain and encourage a population explosion that creates problems for the local authority whose job it is to clear up the mess they make on some of the town's buildings.

The pied wagtail is easy to identify by its bobbing tail.

119

The feral pigeon is descended from the wild rock dove and many of our town flocks are the descendants of ancestors who lived in dovecotes and provided winter food supply for the gentry of the day who could afford such apparent luxury.

However, for the keen observer they are particularly fascinating for the way they take advantage of any situation offering a food source. For instance, in seaside towns they are often seen scavenging along winter beach tidelines and in summer thriving on left-over sandwiches; in inland towns they know where people eat in the open, in parks, squares and along the riverside; around docks, factories and warehouses they find more abundant food. As you watch them, think about how well they have adapted to town life.

The first collared doves arrived in England in 1952 from the Continent where they had spread quite dramatically; in the British Isles they found an ecological niche that resulted in a population explosion that spread them far and wide. They are a successful species because they avoid competition with other pigeons by favouring suburban gardens, villages and highly developed coastal areas. A black half collar around the back of the neck, provides the key to identification.

If you are out at dusk keep an open eye for starling roosts in town buildings. It is a most stirring sight to watch them wheeling and circling against the sunset; you cannot help but wonder how they achieve such perfect unison of movement. With the benefit of subtle sounds, signs and visual signals they perform amazing aerial manoeuvres – just imagine a hundred thousand birds, flying fast and only inches apart wheeling with such perfection, their reaction to and awareness of each other, their consciousness of the flock movement, these momentary decisions synchronized with such amazing sensitivity. Starlings may be regarded as pests for the mess they produce in their roosts, but let us enjoy their gyrations against the evening sky and marvel at their 'flock consciousness'. If you ever have the opportunity to get close to a starling roost, as the birds alight you will experience a heightened awareness of life, for there, so close to you, are a hundred thousand tiny hearts beating in unison, a hundred thousand tiny brains quietening down for the long night as they chatter to each other and to themselves. Occasional brief silences follow and then quite suddenly, as the last glimmer of daylight fades, an absolute and immediate silence settles on the great roost. They have been communicating to each other in ways we are only just beginning to understand. And that is no bad thing. We need to have our own limitations defined and if that is brought about by wildlife, so much the better for us and them. Who better to express this feeling than Henry David Thoreau in *Walden*: 'We need to witness our own limits transgressed, and some life pasturing freely where we never wander.'

Another species that has taken advantage of the man-made canyons and cliffs of buildings is the house martin, especially since the various anti-pollution laws have cleared our towns and cities of smog. The Clean Air Act provided ideal conditions for the increase of insect life and the consequent 'times of plenty' for the birds – especially those aerial feeders like the house martin. Have you ever sat back and watched them as they zoom across your view catching insects? What astonishing eyesight they must possess and what an extraordinary ability to seize such tiny insects in their beaks. If you are fortunate enough to have a pair nesting on a nearby house, watch the nest site for a few minutes, half an hour perhaps. You will be surprised at the number of visits they make to feed their young and if you have a pair of binoculars you will be able to see how they feed their young in sequence – enabling each one to get a fair share and thus avoiding the 'over-stuffing' of a greedy one. A survival technique that helps to ensure a successful brood.

Wherever there are humans, you will find house sparrows, they are so common we almost take them for granted, yet their behaviour is always worth a few minutes' watching. In hot dry weather you will find them dust-bathing in a patch of soil and getting into all sorts of surprising positions as they do so, usually in the company of several others. If you have not seen them at it, but find one or two soup-plate size depressions in the soil, in the park for instance, that is sparrows at work, or perhaps play. The male, in the courting season, is a smart fellow with a black bib and bold markings which he displays to the female and also uses to drive off other males entering his territory. The female is gently submissive, trembling her wings in response to his advances.

Watch them too, as they feed their young, the latter making plenty of noise as they flutter their wings and beg for food. Sparrows have a habit, not exactly endearing to gardeners, of taking certain flower buds such as forsythia in late winter and early spring, the petals of yellow crocuses in spring and – all too

often – you will find them at work on the flower buds of polyanthus, especially where these flowers are concentrated in municipal bedding schemes. Unfortunately for sparrows, they are at great risk from cars, for they feed in gutters and alight on roads to drink at small puddles in the tarmac. The young ones seem to be particularly vulnerable.

Between April and August the swifts will be flying over our houses, their screaming cries echoing out of the summer skies. These are extraordinary birds to observe, for they spend so much of their life on the wing, even sleeping by circling and drifting high above us. Often in our wet, misty summers the parents find difficulty in getting food, for few insects will be on the wing in such poor weather conditions – and consequently the young go hungry.

Watching swifts flying with their young, it is chastening to recall that soon they will set off on that long migration south to sunnier climes and yet return again next summer to delight us. Perhaps those small birds have built-in clocks, triggered by light, day length and countless minute signs quite unintelligible to humans. Perhaps they are able to

Watching sparrows dust-bathing is both amusing and fascinating.

remember landmarks, but that implies most accurate navigation. We know that birds use smell and also the earth's magnetic field and that they are able to navigate by stars, moon and sun, but we still have only the smallest understanding of *how* they do it. By whatever means they navigate they are able to return to the nest site in your town, male and female flying independently and apart – a quite remarkable feat.

So many of us seek the rarities and the unusual when all around us is so much to be enjoyed, every day of the week. Those obvious, yet so often ignored, flowers of the wayside and field are beauties to be cherished, but we see them without observing them, pass them by with hurried steps, unaware of all they have to offer. Take dandelions as an example. It amazes me that not a single plant breeder has developed this flower to grace our borders with its shining suns so beautiful on dull spring days. Spare a moment then and ask yourself the question Jefferies asked when he wrote in *Field and Hedgerow*, one hundred years ago:

What is the colour of the dandelion? It is not yellow, nor orange, nor gold; so you may call it the yellow-gold-orange plant ... perhaps if ten people answered this question they would each give different answers.

Well, what colour is it? Without doubt the

ABOVE:
A noise in the night.

OPPOSITE:
*Spring behaviour of the robin: territorial fighting
(above left); juvenile (above right); feeding the chicks takes most
of the daylight hours (centre); courtship feeding (below right).*

122

common dandelion exists in many forms and there are numerous micro-species, for it has adapted to life under extremely varied conditions from playing fields, grassland and lawns to the mud-splattered verges of the motorways. The flowers are able to set viable seed without fertilization, although they still produce pollen. If you look at those seeds with a hand-lens the intricate beauty is revealed, the design efficiency perfect in its purpose.

Quite recently I collected some dandelion heads and counted the number of seeds per flower and the average was 190. If you care to count the numbers of flowers a single dandelion plant produces in a year and multiply that by 190 you will discover a number close to 20,000! Try it this year. It pays to take a closer look at the leaves. You will find the leaf shapes vary according to the season, the age of the plant, and moisture in the soil. So much variation, so much to see in even the most common of our so-called weeds.

So spare a little time for the dandelion and perhaps, like our observer a hundred years ago, you will discover:

There are a million books, and yet with all their aid I cannot tell you the colour of the May dandelion.

FIELD-WORK

Take a walk around town, looking up, down and around. You might well be surprised at the different birds you see.

Treat yourself to a magnifying lens, a triple, double or single 25mm lens. Use it to look at flowers, moss, lichen and seeds. In your spare time, over a period of several weeks, observe a single species of bird, until you really begin to know something about its habits.

There is probably a local conservation group near you: why not join them. Become active in one of the bird organizations, such as the RSPB, YOC or your county naturalist trust.

DAY OF THE SPIDER WEBS

The autumn dawn had shrouded the town in mist, cold, clammy and so very still, the tiny droplets alighting on every plant and man-made structure in the street. By breakfast time a slow gentle breeze set swirls of vapour curling and moving as the air, slowly warmed by the sun, reabsorbed the droplets and the light grew brighter. Within another hour the mist had gone. But what beauty it revealed, that for too long had passed unnoticed. It was surely 'The Day of the Spider Webs'.

Threads so fine as to be almost invisible, spanned gaps between branches, suspending orb webs as large as dinner plates, which the mist had touched to sparkling beauty. Water diamonds held the sky sunlight in countless tiny globes hanging from every silken thread, and within its glistening form each drop mirrored the world around it. Surely here was wonderful proof of the innate ability of the garden or diadem spider to create such delicate beauty, economy of design and engineering artistry. Here were angles, seemingly of geometric accuracy, parallel lines to grace any drawing-board.

That great observer of spiders W S Bristowe 'often wondered if spiders possessed a sense of direction involving memory' yet he, like other spider watchers, would appear to conclude that spiders are born with their skills and play no part in the learning process during their lives.

On this misty morning, the gossamer displayed truths as old as time, the evolved actions blindly ignoring function. Yet here was near perfection beyond our understanding – one could only wonder at the beauty of it all.

Gossamer webs, frosted with crystals or bejewelled with mist drops always reward a really close look.

USEFUL ADDRESSES

British Butterfly Conservation Society
Tudor House, Quorn, Loughborough, Leics LE12 8AD.
The society encourages interest in and awareness of butterflies and their conservation and fights to save threatened wild habitats. Twice a year it publishes BBCS News. It encourages conservation projects by small groups and individuals through liaison with its branch network throughout the country.

Royal Society for the Protection of Birds
Write for membership to: RSPB, The Lodge, Sandy, Bedfordshire SG19 2DL. Has over 115 reserves comprising 140,000 acres, most open to the public. Members receive the popular colourful magazine *Birds*, free four times a year and have free admission to most of the reserves and are eligible to join a countrywide network of lively members' groups. Members receive details of the wide range of gifts, both mail order and through RSPB shops.

The Young Ornithologists' Club
RSPB, The Lodge, Sandy, Bedfordshire SG19 2DL.
This Junior Section of the RSPB has individual membership for anyone under the age of sixteen. Family membership for any number of brothers and sisters plus Adult Associate membership is also available. Write for details, subscription rates and information on the privileges you gain.

Nature Conservancy Council
Produces some highly informative publications on their national nature reserves. Information and Library Services, Northminster House, Peterborough PE1 1UA.

Men of the Trees
Crawley Down, Crawley, Sussex, RH10 4HL.
They have a family tree scheme, a journal for members. Write for details of membership.

British Mycological Society
In addition to membership the society publishes *The Mycologist*, which is full of information on Fungi. General Secretary, CAB International Mycological Institute, Ferry Lane, Richmond, Surrey TW9 3AF.

British Deer Society
Church Farm, Lower Basildon, Reading, Berkshire RG8 9NH.
With membership you gain *Deer Magazine* (three issues per year). Information service, education programme, training, research and meetings.

The Bird Information Service
Appletree Cottage, Marshside, Brancaster, King's Lynn, Norfolk PE31 8AD.
The monthly magazine *Birding World* brings you the latest birding news, bird-finding articles, current rarity reports and much more. Also offers you Birdcall (0898) 700227 and Birdline the twenty-four-hour rare bird information service. For details of the Birdline numbers and other enquiries phone (0485) 210349.

Marine Conservation Society
9 Gloucester Road, Ross-on-Wye, Herefordshire HR9 5BU.
The society campaigns for marine conservation from sharks to polluted beaches, the dying North Sea, coral reefs and much more. It offers members all kinds of co-operative research projects so that you can really become involved in your own area. Sales brochure of books, posters and gifts.

Field Studies Council
Preston Montford, Montford Bridge, Shrewsbury, SY4 1HW.
Write for their information pack. The council organizes natural history courses in nine centres, for people from all walks of life.

Royal Society for Nature Conservation
22 The Green, Nettleham, Lincoln LN2 2NR.
This is the national association of the forty-eight local wildlife or nature conservation trusts in various counties, and fifty urban wildlife groups.

Institute of Terrestrial Ecology
Monks Wood Experimental Station, Abbots Ripton, Huntingdon PE17 2LS. Tel: Abbots Ripton 381.
The institute organizes a Butterfly Monitoring Scheme in which you might like to participate. It publishes the booklet *Instructions for Independent Recorders*.

FURTHER READING

The following books are recommended, but a browse through a bookshop or local library will reveal many more. Some may now be out of print, but if you can discover them in secondhand bookshops you will find their contents to be as fresh as ever.

GENERAL NATURAL HISTORY

BP Guide to Exploring Britain's Wildlife (David & Charles)

Macmillan's Guide to Britain's Nature Reserves – Hywel-Davies J, Thom V (Macmillan)

The 'New Naturalist' series by Collins provides excellent background reading. A list giving up-to-date availability and prices is available from Natural History Editor, Collins/Harvill, 8 Grafton Street, London W1

The Outdoor Guide to Britain – John Gooders (Webb & Bower)

Out in the Country. Where you can go and what you can do. Booklet from Countryside Commission Publications, 19/23 Albert Road, Manchester M19 2EQ. Free catalogue available, enclose SAE

Publicity Services Branch, Nature Conservancy Council, Northminster House, Peterborough PE1 1UA. Ask for catalogue listing current titles

Collins Guide to the Countryside in Winter – Alastair Fitter and Richard Fitter

RSPB Nature Reserves – Ed Nicholas Hammond, RSPB, (Christopher Helm)

The Grasses, Sedges, Rushes and Ferns of Britain and Northern Europe – Fitter, Fitter and Farrer (Collins)

London's Natural History New Naturalist Library – Richard Fitter (Collins)

The Natural History of Britain and Northern Europe series: *Towns and Gardens, Mountains and Moorlands, Fields and Lowlands, Rivers Lakes and Marshes* (Hodder & Stoughton)

Watching Wildlife – Alan Major (David & Charles)

BIRDS

Where to watch birds in ... (Christopher Helm) Each volume covers three to five counties

Bird Watching in Britain. A Site-by-Site Guide – Nigel Redman and Simon Harrap (Christopher Helm)

Seabirds: an identification guide – revised edition, Peter Harrison (Christopher Helm)

Tracks and Signs of the Birds of Britain and Europe: an identification guide – Roy Brown, John Ferguson, Mike Lawrence and David Lees (Christopher Helm)

What's That Bird? – Peter Hayman and Michael Everett for the RSPB (Christopher Helm)

A Field Guide to the Birds of Britain and Europe – Roger Peterson, Guy Mountford and P A D Hollom (Collins)

A Field Guide to the Nests, Eggs and Nestlings of British and European Birds – Colin Harrison (Collins)

Bird Table Book – Tony Soper (David & Charles)

Owls. Their Natural and Unnatural History – Tony Soper and John Sparks (David & Charles)

A Passion for Birds – Tony Soper (David & Charles)

Bird Habitats of Great Britain and Ireland – Paul Morrison (Michael Joseph)

Birds in your Garden – Tony Soper and Roger Lovegrove (Webb & Bower)

FLOWERS

A Field Guide to the Wild Flowers of Britain and Northern Europe – Fitter, Fitter and Blamey (Collins)

New Generation Guide to the Wild Flowers of Britain and Northern Europe – Dr Alastair Fitter (Collins)

NON-FLOWERING PLANTS

Collins Guide to the Ferns, Mosses and Lichens of Northern Europe – Hans Martin Jahns

Collins Guide to Mushrooms and Toadstools – M Lange and F B Hora

British Seaweeds – Carola M Dickinson (Eyre & Spottiswoode)

FRESHWATER LIFE

A Field Guide to Freshwater Life in Britain and North-West Europe – R S R Fitter and Richard Manuel (Collins)

INSECTS

Dragonflies of Great Britain and Ireland – C O Hammond FRES (Harley Books)

A Field Guide to the Butterflies of Britain and Europe – L G Higgins and N D Riley (Collins)

Colour Identification Guide to Moths of the British Isles – Bernard Skinner (Viking (Penguin))

A Field Guide to the Caterpillars of Britain and Europe – David Carter and Brian Hargreaves (Collins)

A Field Guide to Grasshoppers and Crickets of Britain and Northern Europe – Helko Bellmann (Collins)

A Field Guide to Insects of Britain and Northern Europe – Michael Chinnery (Collins)

MAMMALS

The Natural History of Badgers – Ernest Neal MBE (Christopher Helm)

The Natural History of Otters – Paul Chanin (Christopher Helm)

The Natural History of Squirrels – John Gurnell (Christopher Helm)

Collins Guide to Animal Tracks and Signs – Preben Bang, Preben Dahlstrom

The Mammals of Britain and Europe – Corbet and Ovenden (Collins)

Squirrels in Britain – Keith Laidler (David & Charles)

MARINE LIFE

Collins Pocket Guide to the Seashore – John H Barrett and C M Yonge (Collins)

A Field Guide to Sea Fishes of Britain and N W Europe – Bent M Muus and Peter Dahlstrom (Collins)

A Field Guide to the Mediterranean Seashore – Luther and Fledler (Collins)

Coasts and Estuaries – Richard Barnes (Hodder & Stoughton)

The Living Seashore – Joan M Clayton (Warnes)

MOLLUSCS

A Field Guide to the Land Snails of Britain and N W Europe – Michael Kerney, Robert Cameron and Gordon Riley (Collins)

British Bivalve Seashells – Norman Tebble (Natural History Museum)

British Seashells – Nora F McMillan (Warnes)

REPTILES AND AMPHIBIANS

A Field Guide to the Reptiles and Amphibians of Britain and Europe – N Arnold, J A Burton and D W Ovenden (Collins)

TREES

The Trees of Britain & Northern Europe (new edition) – Alan Mitchell and John Wilkinson (Collins)

ACKNOWLEDGEMENTS

The author is grateful to the following publishers for granting permission to use quotations from their books:

Methuen & Co: *King Solomon's Ring* by Konrad Lorenz.
Thomas Nelson and Sons Ltd: *Fabre's Book of Insects* by Eleanor Doorly.

Quartet Books Ltd: *The Story of my Heart* by Richard Jefferies.
J M Dent and Sons Ltd: *Out of Doors* by Richard Jefferies.
Penguin Books Ltd: (New American Library and Signet Classic) *Walden or Life in the Woods* by Henry David Thoreau.